Equality and the Religious Traditions of Asia

The articles in this volume are part of a project organized by the International Centre for Ethnic Studies (ICES), in co-operation with UNESCO and the United Nations University, on 'Concepts of Equality in the Religious and Cultural Traditions of Asia'.

Equality and the Religious Traditions of Asia

Edited by

R. Siriwardena

 Frances Pinter (Publishers), London.

First published in Great Britain in 1987 by
Frances Pinter (Publishers) Limited,
25 Floral Street
London WC2E 9DS

British Library Cataloguing in Publication Data

Equality and the religious traditions of Asia.
  1. Equality   2. Asia — Religion
  I. Title
  291'.095   BL1032

ISBN 0–86187–660–1

Typeset by Spire Print Services Ltd., Salisbury
Printed by Biddles of Guildford Ltd.

Contents

Introduction

'Jesting Pilate' (as Bacon described him), who asked 'What is truth?'
and would not stay for an answer, could well have given the same
ironic inflection to the question 'What is equality?'. Many people who
will unhesitatingly say they are in favour of equality will have great
difficulty in defining what they mean by the word. Even if they adopt
a blanket definition and declare that the aim of social strivings and
aspirations should be to eliminate all forms of inequality — whether of
race, caste, class or gender — there is the troubling fact that men and
women are not in fact born equal, but that they come into the world
with different natural endowments. One possible answer to this
problem is the view that the equality that is truly decisive is equality of
opportunity, that human endeavours should be directed towards
removing discriminations and barriers of every kind that stand in the
way of each individual realizing his innate potentialities. This is a
traditional liberal answer, and the model of the good society it implies
is one of free competition in which merit will flourish, unhampered by
social handicaps and thwartings. For that very reason, however, it will
be rejected by those who believe that a meritocracy can be just as
exclusive and self-perpetuating as an elite of an older kind. Moreover,
a radical view of equality would be that humane social policies should
seek to redress or compensate for natural as much as man-made
inequalities.

It is probably true that in the real world the movement towards
equality, however defined, will never be more than asymptotic, but to
recognize this is not to detract from its force and significance as an
aspiration and a promise which has motivated human beings in
thinking, action and struggle. But to what extent has this drive
towards equality been time-bound and culture-bound? One of the
central issues that confront the contributors to this volume is that of
the similarities and differences between the values affirmed by the
religious traditions, Eastern in origin, and the modern secular human
rights tradition, initiated by the Western Enlightenment and propa-
gated globally since the American and French Revolutions.

As Dr. Chandra Muzaffar brings out in his introductory essay, all the great world religions were conceived of an underlying common humanity, a spiritual being immanent in human kind, which was the basis for the religious assertion of equality. In its most profound form, this recognition would be achieved in mystical states of insight and illumination. For the saint, arahant, bhakta or sufi, man-made social distinctions would appear as illusions and fetters which had to be cast off in reaching spiritual enlightenment. However, while this consciousness is potentially open to any person, regardless of race, caste, class or gender (and this is why the mystical and contemplative traditions contain an important element of religious egalitarianism), in practice it has been achieved only by a few. At the same time, however, religion manifests itself not only in these rare moments of spiritual transcendence experienced by exceptional persons but also in the everyday practices of worship, ritual and ethical governance of human activity. In this latter, institutionalized realm, religion is incorporated into the culture and social relations of a community; it is part of the ideological heritage that a society inherits from its past and hands down, intact or modified, to its future; and like the rest of a society's ideological apparatus, it can be used as the instrument of the needs and interests of social groups, classes, and national states.

In assessing the concepts of equality in the religious traditions of Asia, as set out in the papers in this volume, it is, therefore, important to remember the historical context of the societies in which these concepts were originally propounded and in which they have been transmitted to later generations. This historical approach is essential if we are to avoid the Eurocentric assumption that there was some genius peculiar to Western culture which enabled it to generate modern conceptions of human rights, or even (as has sometimes been claimed) that it was the Christian affirmation of the absolute reality and permanence of the individual human soul which could alone provide the religious soil in which the secular concepts of human rights could grow. It would be wrong to counter this Eurocentrism with an equally naïve assertion of the self-sufficiency of Eastern cultures. There can be no doubt that the contemporary definition of human rights, in its clarity and comprehensiveness, is fundamentally of Western origin, and that it was the inscription of equality on the banners of the American, French and Russian Revolutions which made it a means of popular mobilization throughout the modern world. However, the explanation for these developments has to be sought not in some inherent superiority in Western civilization but in the fact that, for historical reasons, European society, before any other, was able to generate a middle class who, in advancing their own interests, had to produce an ideology of equality and liberty.

It is relevant here to observe that concepts of equality in both the religious and the secular traditions have been subject to continual modification, evolution and transformation in the course of history. It is true that dominant religious institutions have often been insensitive to inequalities of various social kinds. But the secular human rights tradition has also had to grow through a gradual expansion of its horizons. The concepts of political equality of citizens and the equality of persons before the law, when originally enunciated in Western societies, were still limited by considerations of class, race and gender. The founding fathers of the American Republic who proclaimed that all men were created equal and were equally entitled to life, liberty and the pursuit of happiness included among themselves slave-owners for whom blacks were presumably not 'men' in the terms of the Declaration of Independence. Neither the concepts of liberal democracy nor the humane injunctions of Christ to love one's neighbour prevented European colonizers from oppressing subject peoples. Moreover, even in the heyday of Western liberalism in the nineteenth century, women and the poor were excluded from many of the civic rights to which all 'men' were presumed to be entitled. Economic equality as a human right was little recognized until the rise of socialism, and gender equality continues to be contested even as a principle in many societies. There has been a parallel evolution and broadening of concept and practice in relation to equality within different religious traditions: the process is continuing and incomplete, and involves debate, conflict and ideological struggle.

While a true understanding of the philosophy, outlook and values of religions that had their beginnings in pre-modern societies cannot be achieved without situating them in their original historical contexts, the question arises whether a religious tradition should be judged entirely in terms of the concepts internal to the culture in which it originated. To deny althogether the validity of judging the values of any spiritual or intellectual tradition from a standpoint outside it would be to surrender to a disabling cultural relativism. There are, of course, the dangers to which such a judgment is open to conscious or unconscious prejudices or biases on the part of the observer. But that is no reason why we should not engage in the enterprise of striving to reach a coign of vantage from which we can view different religious and cultural traditions in the light of the human possibilities whose flowering is fostered or limited by them. Such an endeavour is inescapable today when the isolation of cultures has ended and East and West face each other in a mutual cultural encounter.

It is necessary in this introduction to clarify the framework of the workshop at which the first drafts of the papers included in this volume were read. In planning the workshop it was decided that the focus of discussion would be the concepts of and attitudes towards equality in the different religious traditions, as evidenced by their canonical scriptures. The reader needs to bear in mind the textual orientation that the scholars participating in this inquiry were called upon to maintain. Texts are, of course, open to and have been subjected to varying interpretations as they have been used in different historical contexts of time and place. However, in religious communities there has often been a distance between doctrinal tenets and social practice. While these differences are recognized in the papers in this volume, it was not intended that the present study would explore these aspects of religious behaviour in depth. It is also true that a study of heterodox and dissenting religious schools and sects would illuminate some aspects of the quest for equality that lie outside the scope of this volume. Such heterodox religious movements have often been vehicles of expression by rebellious classes and groups in society.

It is hoped that these aspects will receive fuller attention in future researches sponsored by the International Centre for Ethnic Studies. It is relevant to mention here that ICES has already committed itself to a series of programmes, involving both research studies as well as documentary films, on the relations between religion and the lived experience of women in South Asian societies.

Within the self-imposed limits of the present study, however, one can discern the diverse nature of the influences that religion has exerted on the human strivings towards equality in its manifold aspects. The complexity of these influences cannot be contained within any simple formula which sees religion either as the panacea for social evils or as the opium of the people. It is evident from the material contained in this volume that even in the orthodox religious traditions, elements which were supportive of dominant, oppressive social institutions often co-existed with others that were critical, radical and liberating.

The continuing transformations that concepts of equality within the religious traditions are undergoing under the pressures of social change cannot be halted or reversed by a literalism which interprets religion in the light of meanings that have been rendered archaic by historical movement. Religious institutions and communities, in the face of the social revolution for equality that in varying forms and at varying tempos affects all societies today, have to distinguish between those spiritual and moral values in their traditions that are still of relevance and significance and those elements of social ethics and practice that were incorporated in these traditions to serve the needs of social structures that have now been left behind.

It is noteworthy that there has been unanimity among the contributors on the imperatives of equality between races and classes, but some of them had reservations regarding gender equality. Perhaps these reservations are due to the differences in the growth of consciousness in respect of the liberation of women between Western and Asian societies as well as the continuing dominance of male power within religious institutions. However, time will show that this aspect of the egalitarian revolution will be as irresistible in Asia as it is becoming in Europe or America. Against the view that feminism is a Western heresy, it is pertinent to recall that the great Asian mystics in their moments of supreme insight recognized that distinctions of gender, like those of race and class, were among the human illusions and egotisms that had to be shed by the seeker for spiritual liberation. The Saivite devotee Devara Dasimayya wrote in the tenth century:

> if they see
> breasts and long hair coming
> they call it woman,
>
> if beard and whiskers
> they call it man:
>
> but, look, the self that hovers
> in between
> is neither man
> nor woman
>
> O Ramanatha[*]

R. Siriwardena
International Centre for Ethnic Studies,
8 Kynsey Terrace,
Colombo 8,
Sri Lanka.

[*] Translated by A. K. Ramanujan in *Speaking of Siva* (Penguin Books).

1 Equality and the Spiritual Traditions: An Overview

Chandra Muzaffar

One of the most significant similarities in the various spiritual traditions which is of direct relevance to equality is the notion of man's common humanity. It is this common humanity which is the essence of equality in Buddhism, Christianity, Confucianism, Hinduism, Islam and Taoism. Because we are all human beings, we are all the same. It was K'ung Fu-tze who once noted that human beings everywhere are much the same in terms of their basic nature. It is nurture that makes them different. Our human status then, and all that it implies from the point of view of our emotions and impulses, our motives and our urges, is what makes us equal.

This concept of equality, which we shall call the philosophical notion of equality, expressed itself in different ways in the Indo-Aryan and Semitic traditions. (Here again we must remind ourselves that we are using the 'Indo-Aryan' and 'Semitic' labels in a broad, perhaps, superficial sense.) In the Indo-Aryan religions like Hinduism and Buddhism man is equal because all of us are part of the universe, part of an integrated, harmonious whole. There is, in other words, a cosmic notion of oneness, a oneness that renders every atom in that vast expanse a bearer of the universal essence. This universal essence is what equalizes the human race. The Semitic religions — Christianity, Judaism and Islam — also subscribe to a notion of universal oneness. But in their case, equality is more specifically articulated through man's relationship with God. Since man is made in the image of God in Christianity, since man is the viceregent of God in Islam, all human beings are equal in that they share a common Father, the same Creator. Equality lies in common progeny — since we are all children of God.

Common progeny is further reinforced by man's position as the descendant of Adam, a view of creation held by all the Semitic religions. In the Christian scriptures, as in the Quran, reference is made now and then to man's common ancestry as a way of emphasizing the common bond that units humankind.

Out of both these ideas — man as the viceregent of God and man as the descendant of Adam—emerges the concept of man's responsibility on earth. It is a responsibility that all human beings share without distinction or differentiation. It is a responsibility to fulfil God's trust, to carry out God's work. This means — in the words of the Quran — upholding all that is virtuous and fighting all that is evil. In fulfilling God's trust, man discovers yet another element that links him to the rest of humanity.

At this philosophical level, the Taoist notion of equality is perhaps closer to certain strains within Hinduism and the Indo-Aryan tradition in general than it is to the Semitic religions. The Taoist belief in the indissoluble bond between man and nature furnishes the basis for the equality of all that exists within the unity of the universe. Confucianism, the other Chinese religion, also acknowledges the equality of human beings in so far as it recognizes the fundamental indivisibility of human nature — a point that has just been noted.

So far we have looked at equality in its most philosophical sense, as a sort of esoteric idea dwelling in a large conception of man–universe or man–God relationship. But if we examine the various traditions in some depth, we shall discover that their doctrines also embody more specific and sometimes more concrete notions of equality. We shall now analyse some of these notions of equality in a systematic manner.

In most religions, there is a concept of piety, of righteousness that is attainable by anyone. This in itself signifies egalitarianism. For very often these religions maintain that it is righteous conduct — and righteous conduct alone — that distinguishes one human being from another. It is another way of saying that ethnic, religious, class and gender distinctions are secondary. This emphasis upon righteousness as the only distinguishing characteristic that matters in the eyes of God is a vital dimension of Islam. In Buddhism, the attainment of Arhantship is not confined to any particular elite or class. Anyone who can achieve nirvana — and the path to nirvana is open to everyone — is assumed to have reached that stage.

Though Buddhism and Islam, like other religions, see spiritual bliss as something that is available to all, in reality both these traditions have allowed the emergence of a class that claims the privilege of piety. The growth and consolidation of the power of a 'priesthood' is totally repugnant to the pristine traditions of these religions.

The growth of priestly classes — whether monks or rabbis or ulama — must be regarded as antithetical to the ideal of equality contained in the philosophical foundations of the various religions. In this connection, it is interesting to note that the little Christian communities that established themselves in various parts of the Middle East in the earliest years of the religion did not have priests or servants.

Doctrinal rejection of a clergy aside, early Muslim communities, too, were singularly successful in sustaining their spiritual dynamism without the hindering influence of a priesthood. And yet, over the centuries in certain parts of the Muslim world, clerical power has become a daunting reality. Once this happens, the clergy determines morality, laws, the character and conduct of society in such a way that the vast majority of people begin to feel that they have no access to righteousness, no entry to piety. It is this that fosters a sense of inequality.

The same situation obtains as far as the relationship of equality to ethnicity goes. On the one hand, all religions, with perhaps varying degrees of emphasis, espouse the equality of man, irrespective of ethnicity. In Taoism and Buddhism, it has been argued, there is hardly any suggestion of ethnic predispositions since the concern is with universal man in the truest sense. Christianity and Islam too are genuinely universal. Islam, for instance, condemns ethnic prejudice in very strong terms and denounces inequalities brought about by ethnic differentiation.

Yet, in both Islam and Christianity their doctrines themselves embody a concept of an in-group as against an out-group. The in-group of believers as opposed to the out-group of non-believers — whatever the original intention of this distinction — has become a firm religious dichotomy compartmentalizing human beings into irreconcilable types. It is perhaps in Judaism that this dichotomy generates its most serious implications. It expresses itself through the idea of a 'chosen people', which by its very nature subordinates the status of the non-Jews.

Of course, it is possible to interpret the 'chosen people' concept — as progressive Jews have done — to mean affirmation of certain human virtues which good people everywhere are supposed to possess. A 'chosen people', in other words, has no ethnic connotation. Seen in this light, there is perhaps no inequality in the relations among communities in the Judaic doctrine. A similar reinterpretation of what is really meant by other conventional dichotomies between 'believers' and 'non-believers', the 'faithful' and 'infidels', the 'saved' and the 'damned', is perhaps much needed at this stage. What this shows is that the real division is between the good (the believers) and the bad (the non-believers), with good and bad determined solely by the deed one performs rather than the faith one professes.

If it is a question of reinterpretation, then Confucianism, which from certain angles is ethnocentric, can also be viewed differently. It has been said that the well-known phrase of K'ung Fu-tze, 'Within the four seas all men are brothers', is actually a reference to unity and equality among the Chinese. On the other hand, it can also be understood as unity among the whole of humanity, given the then prevailing knowledge of our physical world.

While it is possible to provide varying interpretations of something like ethnicity, religious perspectives on the position of women in society appear to be less ambiguous. At the most general level, in all religions there is a tacit recognition of a woman's equal status since she is after all part of humanity. In some religions equality is accorded in more specific ways. Within the Islamic doctrine, for instance, women enjoy equality in numerous spheres. This includes religious duties, education and reward for labour. As with Islam, Buddhism, too, provides access to women to lofty spiritual statuses such as arhantship. In original Christianity and Taoism there is a remarkable absence of any explicit reference to gender in matters of social rights and responsibilities. Indeed, anthropologists like Marcia Pagels in her *Gnostic Gospels* have shown that, if anything, Christ exhibited in his mission a strong commitment to the position of despised and downtrodden women.

In spite of all this, it is undeniably true that in most religious philosophies there are also evidences of a certain downgrading, even belittling, of women's status. It is apparent that Islam does not place women on an equal footing with men in the realm of public affairs. It nurtures certain views of women's temperament which are clearly unacceptable to modern psychology. Similarly, the Buddha, in a famous discussion with his disciple Ananda, conveyed the impression that there were certain inherent tendencies in a woman's character which made her inferior to man. Even more blunt and blatant descriptions of 'female nature' are found in some of the Hindu traditions.

The denial of an explicit role for women in public affairs in many religious doctrines is one of the more obvious of the political inequities found in the various traditions. In other respects, all the religions, in a rather ambiguous way, allow for people's participation in public affairs. Some of them, it is true, even incorporate ideas which may be described in contemporary language as hinting at the political rights of the ordinary human being. In Buddhism, there is some recognition of the people's duty to rectify wrongdoings. This can be interpreted as providing a certain degree of 'equality' to the common man. Christ's mission, from a progressive perspective, was directed entirely towards strengthening the position of the powerless. In the process — it can be argued — he sought to achieve a more equal society. The same would be true of Islam and Judaism. Both religions make it an obligation upon the believer in God to fight political oppression. The liberation of the oppressed to which the Hebrew prophets committed their lives — the most notable of whom was Prophet Isaiah — invariably enshrined the noble aim of creating a just and egalitarian society. As for the Prophet Muhammad, he not only gave concrete meaning to political equality by placing ruler and ruled on the same level as far as the law was concerned, but he also equalized the two by making the former accountable to the latter and by making the latter the sole judge and arbiter of the former.

Be that as it may, in Islam, as in other religions of antiquity there is a certain aura that surrounds the leader, sanctified as it were by doctrine. The leader is invariably perceived as the embodiment of extraordinary attributes. It is his moral equalities — more than anything else — that determine the well-being of society. This is a veiw which is of course incongruous with present-day knowledge of the complexity of social forces that decide the fate of a community.

The major flaw in the perpetuation of an almost sacral notion of a leader or ruler is that it makes the led or the ruled acutely conscious of their inequality. More than that, it can create a situation where everyone is unquestioningly loyal to the leader. This could encourage the ruler to abuse his power, especially if punishment for such abuse, according to the scriptures, comes from Heaven rather than the people. Confucianism is an example of a doctrinal system which, unwittingly perhaps, legitimizes such abuse of power — in spite of what it says about reciprocal obligations between ruler and ruled. In various schools of thought within Hinduism there is much more evidence of the exercise of arbitrary authority on the part of kings and emperors which sometimes led to immense human misery and sorrow. What is unfortunate is that the unfettered power of the ruler, in contrast to the shackled powerlessness of the ruled, as found in the religious doctrines, was often the ideological basis for such wanton cruelty.

Just as there is both equality and inequality in the political dimension of most religious philosophies, so are there these two contradictory tendencies in the economic sphere. Many of the orthodox schools in Hinduism and Confucianism may not subscribe to the idea of equality between different economic and social classes, but Judaism, Christianity, Islam and even Taoism give considerable emphasis to egaliterian ideals. Judaism even calls upon its adherents to undertake to redistribute their wealth equitably at certain intervals in time. This is to ensure that disparities are reduced to the minimum and access to resources is equalized. We have already been exposed to Christianity's compassion for the poor. In this connection, it is worth noting that biblical teachings are very much opposed to the accumulation of wealth and the acquisition of riches. Islam has the same aversion to accumulation and acquisition. It, too, believes in a society where there is neither poverty nor exploitation — as stated in one of the *hadith's* (sayings of the Prophet Muhammad). Besides, the Quran enunciates the circulation of wealth among the masses so that the advantages that accrue from it are not confined to a few.

In spite of these egalitarian moral injunctions, Islam — like Christianity and the other great religions — appears to accept disparities in the control of wealth as an inevitable element in the social panorama. One gets the impression that it is with the help of the rich that the poor will be able to save themselves. This is what has led conservative Muslims and Christians to argue that inequalities are natural, that they are part of God's plan.

It we reflect upon what has been discussed so far, it appears that there is a broad, general concept of equality, as part of an overall philosophy of man in most of the spiritual traditions, which expresses itself in specific spheres such as politics and ethnic relations in some of the religions. This is where there is some variation from religion to religion. At the same time, in almost all the traditions there seems to be doctrinal acceptance of inequalities in some form or other.

Is it because of these doctrinal inequalities that equality is often perceived in both Western and many Eastern socities as a human value upheld more by the secular rather than the religious tradition? Is this also why the quest for equality as an essential element in the struggle for human rights is invariably linked to the West — since the East is not only the birthplace of all the great religions but also that part of the world where religions continue to exert tremendous influence in the lives of people? Both these questions are worth exploring in some depth.

Doctrinal inequalities are perhaps part of the explanation. To understand how they affect the quest for equality one has merely to contrast the scriptures with the Declaration of Human Rights or the Covenants on economic and social rights and political and civil rights. The latter are explicit and unambiguous when it comes to the question of equality in comparison to the former. The rights of the individual in the political and economic life of his community or the rights of women and minorities, for instance, are lucidly articulated, and for that reason, serve as clear, precise guidelines for social action. It is, of course, foolish to suggest that this should also be the case with the religious traditions, for their purpose is something else, as we have already indicated in this analysis. Nevertheless, the contrast gives us some idea of why it is the secular tradition — out of which grew the various United Nations proclamations referred to — that appears to be more forthright in its commitment to equality.

A more important reason for this difference is perhaps related to the interpretations of the scriptural texts and the interests of the interpreters. For the great spiritual traditions — as we have shown quite clearly — do embody a moral concern for equality. If they had been interpreted in such a way that the progressive dimension of all the perennial values they enshrined had emerged and dominated human thought and action, then perhaps equality would have been understood as it should be. We have already observed that, except for rare moments in history, this did not happen. As societies inspired by the teaching of illustrious prophets established themselves and became stable and secure, a conservative mood set in. The new class of priests who interpreted the teachings justified and rationalized what were in fact actual social inequities through often fragmented, sometimes distorted, references to the doctrines. Instead of trying to understand the holistic spirit, the total philosophy behind sublime words, they became obsessed with the utterances themselves, which of course provided some support, now and then, as we have pointed out, to the perpetuation of inequalities in the real world of social relationships. Need we emphasize that, in most religions, the importance of equality would only surface if the all-encompassing philosophy of man — rather than doctrinal particularities — is given the prominence it deserves?

Why the priests failed to provide such an interpretation it is not difficult to comprehend. It is quite conceivable that they lacked the depth of knowledge and the breadth of vision which were among the outstanding characteristics of the prophets and great mystics — human beings who were truly 'pure in heart'. It is from these divinely inspired sources that we have learnt so much about the oneness of man, the unity of humankind within which nestles the idea of equality. Unable to appreciate this concept of universal oneness, small-minded priests, with their partial grasp of truth, have succeeded in propagating dichotomies which, in the end, have legitimized inequalities between religions, communities, classes and sexes.

But it was more than a question of knowledge, or the lack of it. The priests interpreted the religious texts the way they did because it served their interests to do so. To highlight inequality and to camouflage equality in the scriptures was one way of ensuring their own dominance over their followers. It helped to justify their unequal status, their unequal access to knowledge, to power, and sometimes to wealth. Indeed, their misinterpretation of the doctrines not only placed them beyond challenge but also endowed them with an aura of sacredness which elevated them to 'immortals' in relation to the masses who listened to them with awe and followed them without question.

Equally important, the priests were part and parcel of the elite stratum of society. Often they worked for kings and princes who were determined to maintain the wide chasm that separated elites from the masses. Societies where power is wielded through unequal structures will need ideologies to rationalize disparity and discrimination. Relgion in many traditional societies played the role of such an ideology. The priests were the ideologues. It was their duty to keep the system going, to ensure that the elites remained in power. And the ruling elites knew that nothing could threaten their status to the same degree as a movement for equality among ordinary people.

From our analysis it is apparent that the structure of traditional societies, elite interests, the position of the priestly class and its orientation were more decisive influences in inhibiting religion from emerging as a channel for the quest for equality than the doctrinal factor as such. It follows from this that doctrinal deficiencies are not the main reason why equality has come to be associated with the West and the secular tradition.

It has more to do with the way in which the concept of equality developed in recent times. There is a need to understand this development so that we will have a better appreciation of how spiritual traditions can relate to an eternal value that acquired its contemporary characteristics as a result of a different historical experience.

The starting-point is post-Renaissance Europe. The key factor was the rise of a whole class whose very survival and success depended upon its ability to secure equal status for itself. A unique juxtaposition of circumstances made that quest a turning-point in man's history.

As a result of the crusades and the new opportunities for trade and industry provided by them, merchant capital and a merchant class made their presence felt in the feudal Europe of the Middle Ages. Partly because of the protracted crusades, partly because of changes in the agricultural system in Europe and the growth of small towns and new industries, these merchants were in an advantageous position to strengthen their economic base to such an extent that they soon enjoyed relative autonomy.

What secured their autonomy, however, was their command over science and the new technical skills necessary for the further development of commerce, industry and transportation in a changing Europe. A great deal of this knowledge was obtained via the crusades, for Islamic civilization was, at that time, the most advanced in science and technology. There was another point of contact between medieval Europe and Islam. This was through Spain and parts of Portugal which were also occupied by Muslim caliphates. In some ways, the Muslim kingdoms of the Iberian peninsula were even greater centres of learning and culture than Damascus or Cairo in that period of history.

The knowledge obtained from Islamic civilization, which in turn had absorbed a lot of ideas from earlier Chinese, Hindu, Greek and Roman civilizations, was, in a sense, a new type of knowledge. It was no longer the speculative 'science' of the past. For between the eighth and twelfth centuries, Islam had pioneered methods of experimentation and procedures for deduction and verification. It had already begun to give importance to empirical research in the investigation of physical and social phenomena. Islam, in a nutshell, had discovered modern science — as Robert Briffault acknowledges in his *The Making of Humanity*. It was this empirical, investigative, experimental science that inspired the development of a vast array of techniques in certain parts of the Muslim world. Post-Renaissance Europe built upon this scientific foundation. It developed it further and provided it with a dynamic impetus, brought about to some extent by its control of new trade routes and its discovery of new sources of wealth. Indeed, as Islamic civilization declined from the fifteenth century onwards, because of a whole variety of factors which need not concern us here, it was Europe that emerged as the centre of the new science and technology.

The control that the new merchant class exercised over knowledge

— apart from its economic strength — was what made it potentially so powerful. It became the nucleus of a whole new class which included scientists, artists and writers, in addition to bankers, financiers and insurance operators. This was the beginning of the European bourgeoisie. Given its growing importance, it was bound to come into conflict with the feudal class and the Catholic Church, who reinforced each other's power. Political power was, in fact, still in the hands of these two groups. They were able to determine the rules pertaining to trade and the establishment of commercial enterprises and industries, just as they determined taxes for the bourgeoisie. This is why the bourgeoisie wanted political power, since it saw the feudal class and the church as inimical to its interests. Equality therefore became the leading slogan of the bourgeoisie. Equal political rights and the freedom to do business without hindrance became its major concerns. This explains why so many of the intellectual masterpieces from the sixteenth to the eighteenth centuries, such as John Locke's *Two Treatises of Government* or Montesquieu's *Spirit of the Laws*, were actually devoted to bourgeois rights presented as human rights.

The bourgeoisie's passionate commitment to equality — albeit equality for the sake of its own class — drew its intellectual succour from traditions outside medieval Europe and medieval Christianity. Although there were egalitarian movements in medieval Europe, some of them deriving their inspiration from Christianity, they had very little impact upon the elites, especially the religious elites. There is no doubt that Hellenic thought, with its emphasis upon equality, was one of the important sources of influence. For ideas from Hellenic civilization, transmitted through Islam, played a significant role in the European Renaissance. Similarly, ideas on equality from Islamic philosophy — ideas which can be gleaned from the earlier part of this chapter — had a considerable impact upon the Europe of that period. Ideas on the rights of minorities and women, equality among occupational categories and the importance of raising the status of the poor and downtrodden, were some of the influences that emanated from Islam. M. N. Roy, in his *The Historical Role of Islam*, has shown how these and other Islamic influences upon human civilization had contributed immensely towards the progressive development of man.

However, it was not because of ideas from outside but because of the internal dynamic of the European situation, that the quest for equality reached yet another stage. After the bourgeoisie had secured equality and established its power, its exploitation of the working class (the proletariat), coupled with the almost total denial of rights to the proletariat, persuaded a segment of the European intelligentsia to examine the concept of equality from the perspective of the masses. It was this process which began with the humanistic, socialist writings of the early decades of the nineteenth century and which culminated eventually in an all-embracing philosophy of human rights in the last few decades of the twentieth century. Of course, even in Europe and the West, these rights have yet to be realized in their totality. Nevertheless, at the level of ideas, human rights — and the concept of equality which is germane to them — are now expounded in relation to the status of the ordinary human being. It is no longer linked to either the privileges of a particular group or the aspirations of a particular class. In that sense, the philosophy of human rights today has repudiated all divisions and dichotomies. It is truly a universal philosophy.

As it is universal in the ideational sense, so it has become global in the geographical sense. While ideas related to human rights seeped into the non-Western world in the latter period of colonial rule, the actual diffusion of human rights ideals on a global scale is a much more recent phenomenon. It is, in a way, a product of the trans-nationalization of Western culture and Western ideals. This is why the endeavour to seek equal rights for the poor or the ruled or minorities or women is often labelled as the pursuit of a Western ideal.

Is it fair to label the pursuit of equality in that way? How should we relate to a universal value which has undoubtedly been conditioned by the social setting in which it developed in the last few centuries? To start with, there are certain aspects of the European experience which are, in fact, part of a universal process. Our study has shown, for instance, how both Hellenic and Islamic civilizations contributed to the development of equality in post-Renaissance Europe. This is how it has always been in the history of ideas. An eternal, universal idea, however evident the attributes of a particular age, will also manifest characteristics which transcend time and place. It is these characteristics which enable an idea to grow from age to age, to reveal, in the fullness of time, its inner meaning and message. This is why equality as it developed in secular, Western society is not entirely alien to religious, non-Western societies.

Besides, if we look at the specific content of equality, reflected in the rights of individuals in various spheres of contemporary Western society, we will realize that there are many similarities with the spiritual doctrines we have analysed in this essay. Equality in relation to a person's right to life, liberty and security, for instance, is highly cherished in both the secular and the religious traditions. In this connection, it is interesting to observe that the notion of equality, and indeed, a number of the rights enunciated in the Universal Islamic Declaration of Human Rights of 1981, are almost identical to those contained in the Universal Declaration of Human Rights of 1948 — though the philosophical basis of the former is religious while the philosophical basis of the latter is secular. A couple of examples will suffice. Both state that 'no one shall be subjected to arbitrary arrest, detention or exile'. Both agree that 'every person is entitled to receive education'. There are other similarities pertaining to freedom of association, freedom of opinion, the right to work, consent before marriage and so on. This merely goes to show that when some of the values and principles embodied in religion are made explicit in terms of rights and freedoms, the parallels with the secular tradition in relation to human rights become apparent.

Of course, this does not mean that there are no differences. Neither does it mean that everything in the European quest for equality would be applicable to the Asian peoples. It is wrong, for instance, to believe that equality can be advanced in our socieities only if we go through similar historical stages — that, in other words, the bourgeoisie must struggle against the feudal class, and the proletariat against the bourgeoisie before the rights of the human being are secured in full. It need not work this way in every case. There may be a leap in history, or various stages may overlap with one another. This is partly because the feudal class in many non-Western societies was never feudal in the classical manorial sense and therefore did not exercise the power and authority of the kings and princes of medieval Europe. Besides, colonialism — which was not part of Europe's experience — had sometimes liquidated feudal structures, thus averting a clash between feudal interests and the local bourgeoisie. In other instances, feudal ruling houses have been so severely circumscribed that their continued presence is largely symbolic. Similarly, how is it possible to talk of a local bourgeoisie struggling for equality when the circumstances of colonial rule and the situation in the post-colonial period have made it so easy for the middle class — the local bourgeoisie, if you like — to establish its power? Indeed, if anything, it is the usurpation of the rights of others by the middle class through the state that is the reality in many non-Western societies. Nothing dramatizes as vividly the contrast between these societies and the bourgeoisie in Europe than the manner in which the state, which embodies middle-class interests, has succeeded in absorbing business and industry and the economy as a whole into its arena of authority. How then can we expect equality to be accomplished through a similar historical process? Why then should we model our own struggle for equality upon historical premises which are valid only for the European experience?

By the same token, we should not hold on to the belief that the quest for equality has to come into conflict with religion and the church since that is the way it happened in Europe. Neither is it right to argue that equality is possible only if it is based upon secular foundations.

Our own diagnosis of the spiritual traditions has indicated quite clearly that equality is part of those doctrines. Even if there are certain doctrinal inadequacies, a progressive reinterpretation of the scriptures guided by their underlying values will establish the paramount significance of equality. Why then should one see the struggle for equality as something that has to happen outside religion?

In any case, Christianity today is proving the point that it can take place within religion. There is a great deal of concern with equality and the question of human rights in general. Jesus' mission — as we have seen — is now being offered as evidence of the religion's commitment to equality and justice for all, especially the poor and downtrodden. And yet it is the same Christian faith, and the same institution of the Church, which once denied the rights of the people. It is its role, its relationship with the masses, that has changed. This indicates that religion can become an important channel in the quest for equality — provided it is properly understood and its teachings are supported by just social structures which give real meaning to human dignity.

In fact, it is even possible to suggest that if the struggle for equality is divorced from religion, it could have adverse consequences for man in the long run. For by locating man at the centre of the universe, by making man the be-all and end-all of his own struggle to assert his own rights, the secular tradition has, in a sense, distorted the meaning of equality in at least two ways.

First, since man is the end goal, the ultimate, the values associated with him, be they justice or freedom or equality, also become ends in themselves. This means that the pursuit of equality — in our case — becomes such an inordinate obsession that it even refuses to accept that there are certain aspects of life that cannot be made equal. For while one can equalize access to resources, equalize social structures, equalize economic and political relationships, one cannot possibly equalize human motivations, impulses and aspirations. This seems simple and logical enough, and yet if one examines nationalization in many communist states, one realizes that in the drive to equalize incomes and statuses, there is a tendency to ignore the fact that as long as people differ in their inclinations and orientations, there are bound to be differences in attainment and achievement. One cannot equalize beyond a certain point. Similarly, in ideologically different, though also secular, liberal democratic societies the desire for equality between the sexes has, in some cases, led to a subtle, sophisticated imposition of uniformity. That there are temperamental, apart from physical, differences between the sexes that militate against the creation of a unisex society is something that is arrogantly brushed aside by dogmatic advocates of sexual equality. There is an unwillingness to try to understand that the man–woman distinction, a certain degree of differentiation in roles, may be fundamental for the psychological well-being of society.

Second, when man is seen in isolation from the totality of existence, when he is separated from larger transcendental goals and purposes, it is inevitable that his values will also be viewed in fragmented, compartmentalized perspectives. What this implies is that, though in theory there may be some conception of values in their integrated wholeness, in reality each value would be emphasized for its own importance. Thus, by stressing equality alone or freedom alone, the secular West has failed to appreciate the interrelationships among diverse and sometimes divergent values which are all part of a composite whole. It is an integrated unity, a universe, that cannot be taken apart, or put into separate slots. It is this 'taking apart' that is partly responsible for the crisis in values in the West today. More specifically this means that the pursuit of equality does not mean repudiating the need for authority. It means that the insistence upon equality need not lead to the loss of excellence. Each and all of these values have their rightful places in the total scheme of things. Or, to state the point in yet another form, equal rights for man and women should not result in the collapse of the family as society's fundamental unit of harmony.

Because none of the spiritual philosophies regard man as an end in himself, there is some protection from the adverse consequences of the secular conception of equality. In the spiritual philosophies, man has a transcendental purpose, it may be to discover the divine in him — as in some traditions — or it may be to serve God — as in other traditions. But in both cases, the goal transcends his human existence. Man reaches out beyond man. There is a seeming paradox here. Man is important and yet unimportant. For on the one hand, it is man who is capable of divinity, who holds God's trust; on the other hand, what he attempts to discover, what he tries to serve, is bigger than himself. Since, in this conception man's situation is humbler, since he is not the ultimate, his values are only means towards a greater end. Equality is not an end in itself. Discovering the divinity in man is; serving God is.

Also, in the spiritual philosophies, man is part of nature, part of the universe, part of eternity. There is an enduring spiritual life beyond what is immediate and ephemeral. It is not so with secular thought where man is pitted against nature, against the universe, against eternal existence. Since man is part of a greater harmony, his values are also part of a larger tapestry of interwoven values. and therefore it is not equality by itself, or freedom by itself or solidarity by itself, that matters. They are all part of an all–encompassing spiritual world-view which has both purpose and meaning.

It will be recalled that, at the beginning of this eassay, it was suggested that in the spiritual traditions there is a philosophical notion of equality which locates that value within a larger spiritual philosophy of man. What this analysis has shown is that there is a need for such a philosophy to guide the struggle for equality. By placing equality, or any other value for that matter, within such a framework, we are in fact spiritualizing what is currently seen as a secular value. Indeed, it is only by spiritualizing the struggle for equality that it will capture the imagination of the ordinary human being who, in the ultimate analysis, remains deeply spiritual.

2 Equality and Inequality in the Hindu Scriptures

Surabhi Sheth

I

The traditional Hindu society is described as a hierarchical society. Hierarchy is identified as the central organizing principle of society which governs all relationships: between individuals, between groups and even among gods, heavenly bodies, trees and plants. Any attempt, therefore, to reconstruct the concept of equality from the Hindu scriptures may appear as plain rationalization or at best an apologia. This is especially so when an attempt is made to extricate a particular value like equality from the web of complex moral and religious concepts developed over centuries not merely as abstract philosophical formulations but as active principles, rules and codes that determine behaviour and create concrete institutional structures that have shown formidable durability and resilience. My attempt in this chapter, therefore, will be to examine the embedding of the value in the larger context of Hindu thought and practices.

Consideration of a discrete value, such as equality, in a tradition like Hinduism poses several analytical difficulties. Firstly, the Hindu thinkers and law-givers themselves assiduously avoid absolutizing any particular value. Even the supreme value of *mokṣa* (salvation) can be achieved only by pursuing the apparently contradictory values of *artha* (wealth) and *kāma* (pleasure) by a *gṛhastha* (housholder) when these pursuits are carried out in accordance with the rule of *dharma*. Even the highest virtue, *dharma*, cannot be acquired by negating basic human motives like the pursuit of wealth or pleasure, even though such pursuits appear intrinsically non-virtuous. It is the harmony of motives and a sense of balance and propriety which *dharma* brings to these pursuits which is more important than absolutizing abstract virtue or wealth or pleasure. As Manu has said, wisdom is to be found in a harmonious combination of the three prime motives of human nature. 'There are those who declare', he says, 'that the highest good, here below, consists in virtue (*dharma*) and in wealth (*artha*); [others say it consists in] pleasure (*kāma*) and wealth, or in virtue alone, or in wealth alone; but the true opinion is that it consists in the conjunction of all the three' (II.224).

Secondly, the importance of a value, according to Hindu law-givers, does not lie in its abstraction but only in the context in which it is embodied. Its importance or worth may vary from time to time (*kāla*) and from place to place (*deśa*). No value can be universalized or absolutized as good for all times and all regions. Even *dharma* cannot be invested with such universal meaning. Bhīṣma says in the *Mahābhārata* 'what is *dharma* in one place may be *a-dharma* in another and what is *a-dharma* in one place may be *dharma* in another'.[1] This orientation provides for flexibility and adaptation of rules with change in time, but it also makes the analytical task of our enquiry difficult. Because of the contextuality of rules and codes of ethics it is always possible to come up with contradictory quotations from the same text to prove or disprove a point.

Thirdly, it is difficult to trace the growth of a discrete value, because Hindu historiography and eschatology do not recognize chronology of events or their linear progression. History (*itihāsa*) for the Hindus is a narrative (*vṛttānta*) of the past in the form of events, stories and legends aimed at exemplifying or preaching (*upadeśa*) human pursuits of *dharma*, *artha*, *kāma* and *mokṣa*.[2] So history's explicit purpose of serving the needs of the present is unapologetically recognized by the Hindus. Hence biographies are created from the values the subject upheld and preached, not from the actual life he or she lived, for example, Mira, Kabir and Surdas. Chronologies have no relevance, for events are considered to be repetitious in nature and only symbolize the character of the *yuga* in which they take place. And the *yugas* change from a better to a worse stage till they come full circle. In such a cyclical view of history, as opposed to the modern linear view, a particular state of society is viewed as a 'fall' from a higher stage, rather than a progress from an earlier lower stage. So, when the occupational and social differentiations take place in society or when it is threatened by external forces (invasions, atheistic ideologies or alien cultures), making the working of the established social and ethical codes difficult, the anxiety of the Hindu law-givers is to hold back the 'fall'. They then tend to devise harsher punishments for violations, and rules that further segmentalize the groups by making special and elaborate rules for each segment. (Notice the change in rules of reward and punishment from Gautama, Baudhāyana and Āpastamba to Manu, for instance.) It is only when they find it difficult to hold back the inevitable 'fall' that the new commentators and law-givers make the codes more liberal and flexible. (Notice the change from Manu to Yājñavalkya and to Bṛhaspati.)

In any event, for the law-givers when they devise more and more inequitable and discriminatory rules for different segments of the society, inequality is not a *cause célèbre* but a recognition of the situation of coping with the downward movement of the wheel of history (*yuga-cakra*). If we respect the terms intrinsic to the self-definition of ancient Hindus, any inquiry into a discrete value like equality cannot be detached from its wider philosophical context, or from its locus in time and place.

It is with the above view in mind that I shall try to delineate the concept of equality with reference to some broader and more fundamental concepts and principles governing the traditional Hindu society, namely the concepts *dharma* and *karma*. These concepts in my view have a direct bearing on the forms in which Hindu ideas and concepts on equality and inequality are manifested. These concepts have retained their centrality till today in folk memory and language. In my delineation I shall base my observations (as I have done so far) mainly on the *sūtras*, *dharmaśastras* and epic–Puranic literature, for it is in this literature that the continuity of present–day practices and problems can be traced, especially those related to the issues of equality and inequality, stability and disorder, social oppression and human rights.

A large part of our understanding of the past is the function of categories we apply to understand it. More often than not, such categories are neither intrinsic to the society we study nor are they such objective, universal and value–free categories as is often assumed or claimed, especially by social scientists. In fact such absolute categories are simply not available to us. The categories and modes of understanding that we apply in understanding any society in the past, or a society which is not our own, are inevitably constructs based on our cognition rooted in the experience, socialization and history of our society. That is exactly how the Hindu law–givers like Manu understood and pronounced on the non–Aryan speaking societies; and that is how the Western rulers and scholars applied categories to understand Indian society. In what follows, I shall attempt to elaborate the terms and concepts used by the ancient Hindu thinkers and law–givers in their expositions and commentaries. My attempt would be to unfold the internal logic of reasoning implicit in their theories of Hindu social organization, and to see how they relate to the modern concepts of equality and inequality.

II

Central to the Hindu social thought are the twin concepts of *dharma* and *karma* as constituting the organizing principles of the social order. Let me briefly explicate these concepts with a view to delineating the Hindu ideal of society as it was crystallized by the time of the *smṛtis* and the epic–Puranic literature. My purpose here is to describe these principles as *ideals* expounded by the Hindu law-givers. Indeed, like all ideals, they were imperfectly followed in reality and were in course of time subjected to such aberrations and distortions that, as we shall see later, the *smṛtikāras'* view of *dharma* and *karma* was severely challenged and new interpretations were offered by the several non-Brahmanic schools of thought.

Dharma

The *Dharmaśāstra* theory of the caste system, which says that status (*varṇa*) is determined by birth (deeds of the past life or lives) and that differential duties (*varṇadharma*) are assigned to each status by the rule of *dharma*, is generally interpreted by sociologists in terms of the hierarchy principle. This is often done without considering place (*deśa*), or time-period (*kāla*) considerations, which for the Hindu thinkers and law-givers are of vital significance in the working of the general principle of *dharma*.

In fact, hierarchy is not the concept used by the Hindu law-givers to describe their own society. They do not propound or uphold hierarchy as a principle of social organization. They also do not talk in terms of a rigid structure or ideal, valid for all times, comprising the 'upper' and 'lower' beings, or strata. Society for them is maintained not by what we today call 'hierarchy', but by order (*ṛta* or *dharma*). *Dharma* to them does not signify hierarchy *per se*, but a natural order that maintains everything in a state of harmony and balance, internally within the individual self and externally in the society and the universe at large. It thus minimizes conflicts and maximizes co-operation so that individual salvation becomes possible for all. Hence the relationship between the strata and orders, which, according to the ancient Hindu law-givers, are the given eternal features of any social organization, has to be governed by the principle of rights enforced by use of secular power, or by the intrinsic highness of the 'high' and lowness of the 'low'; that is, not by the principle of 'hierarchy'. Hierarchy is maintainable only through use of external force and coercion which by its nature is conflictual and disintegrative. When *dharma* is the basis of the social order, hierarchy becomes dispensable if it creates conflict and disorder (*a-dharma*). Society, for the ancient Hindus, was thus governed by the rule of *dharma* (order, duty) which transcends hierarchies.

Relationships between different groups, and between the individual and the collective are ordered through the notion not of 'rights' but of 'duties'. The only right conceded, be it to an individual or a group, is the right to compel the concerned parties to perform their duty. No intrinsic rights are enjoined on one's status. But duties are firmly enjoined on one's status. Hierarchy can never constitute its own justification. *Dharma* alone was regarded as self-contained, requiring no justification outside itself.

As against the Hindu law-givers' view of their own society, Western social science and historiography identifies hierarchy as the central organizing principle of Hindu society. This is because from the time the West approached and established its rule over Hindu society equality came to be regarded by Western scholars as the central value of their own civilization. All that they observed of Hindu society was contrasted with their own values. For them, following the Cartesian dichotomy and later applying the Levi-Straussian principle of binary opposition, the opposite of equality was hierarchy. Hence the notion of hierarchy as the central principle of the Hindu social organization. This indeed made sense to Western scholars but not to the Hindus. As we have seen, for the Hindus, the intrinsic principle governing society is *dharma* and not hierarchy. For Hindus, if they must use such dichotomies, the opposite of *equality* is not *hierarchy* but *order*, and the opposite of *dharma* (duty) is not right but licence *swacchanda* or *swecchācāra*.

Linear progression and the dichotomous mode of viewing reality is alien to the Hindu mind. The primary preoccupation — it could even be termed obsession — of the Hindu law-givers is stability, harmony and the maintenance of order, not through the use of secular power of a political authority or through any system of balances and checks, defined in terms of 'rights' of individuals and groups, but by the rule of *dharma*. The rule of *dharma* sought to regulate society by enjoining duties on individuals and groups. And the ultimate sanction for the duties enjoined by *dharma* derives from the burden of *karmas* which each individual carries from past lives and would like to throw off by performing good deeds in this life. Understanding of good deeds is internalized through gradual processes of socialization: learning from history (epics, *Purāṇas* and so on), performance of rites according to the prescribed scriptural codes, following examples of 'good' men participating in collective rites and ceremonies, and following what is customarily considered good: *sadācāra*, *sistācāra*, and *síla*. *Dharma* as derived from these sources maintains itself and its survival does not depend on external secular agencies. In fact it is *dharma* which upholds the 'secular order'. It sustains itself because, manifesting the natural order of things, it is valid in itself.

'*Dharma*', in the *Mahābhārata*, 'is the main stay of the entire world, everything is established in *Dharma*. *Neither the state nor the King, neither the mace (daṇḍa) nor the mace-bearer (daṇḍika) govern the people, it is only by dharma that people secure mutual protection.*'[3] Clearly the terms of such an exposition do not indicate inequality or hierarchy as the basic principle of Hindu social organization. Hierarchy loses its sanction the moment it comes to be in conflict with *dharma*. It is worth noting in this context that Gandhiji's argument for rejecting *Dharmaśāstras*, that is, if they approved of 'untouchability', was based on the notion of *dharma* or the principle of natural justice which did not admit any ritual disabilities of a social group.

Karma

Related to *dharma* is the concept of *karma*. This concept also, in the Western perspective, is seen as the Hindu doctrine of inequality. This view, widely shared by Westernized Indians, is best illustrated in the words of a Scottish missionary John McKenzie. The doctrine of *karma*, he said, 'is responsible for the backwardness of the people of India. . . [by which] good and evil are thought in terms of act rather than of character. . . . [Being a fatalistic concept,] it does nothing to solve the problem of inequalities of human fortunes.' And, it 'justifies the seeming injustices of life . . . and is incompatible with the belief in the possibility of the forgiveness of sins', and hence, 'the concept lacks justification on moral grounds' (McKenzie 1922, pp. 224–32).

For the Hindus, the concept of *karma* was an epochal discovery that explained the differentiations, inequalities and inconsistencies between action and its results; the relationship between which cannot be seen in a direct one-to-one manner. For them it removed an inconsistency in the theory of *dharma* which could not explain why even good men and women practicing *dharma* failed, in certain cases, to attain in their lives the happiness their acts merited, while others, indulging in evil acts, lived happily. Over time, when inequalities emerged as a result of the changes in the occupational structure, this explanation, as we shall see later, served as a justification for injustices arising from the changes in the social order.

The root of both concepts, *dharma* and *karma*, can be traced in the Vedic concept of *ṛta*, 'a course of things', to which men, gods and the entire universe are subject: a straight, direct line which runs through the entire universe and determines the course of nature and the moral order of society. (*Source Book of Indian Philosophy*, pp. 25–27). This was the Vedic concept of an orderly universe governed by laws which did not admit of any arbitrariness. Even the whims or fancies of gods were powerless to change it. In brief, it defined a correct course of action for every one — human beings, gods, heavenly bodies and natural forces. It is law made neither by man nor gods. It is a natural order of things.

In the later part of the Vedic period, in the times of the *brāhmaṇas*, from being a concept of cosmic law, *ṛta* became a concept associated with the performance of rites and rituals in the correct prescribed manner. So the natural–moral order of *ṛta* became the system of rules and sacrificial rites that determined the roles and behaviour of individuals. This gave a special role to a class of people (the *brāhmaṇas* skilled in the knowledge of carrying out sacrificial rites (*karmakāṇḍa*). And thus *brāhmaṇas* acquired a sanctity and even divinity. Their role became that of a mediator between humans on the one hand and the gods and the cosmic order on the other. Only they knew the rites (*ṛta*) — the line which joins the world, the gods and the universe. They alone could invoke it through sacrifices to intercede with the gods concerning human affairs and obtain boons from them. The gods acquired the powers to confer boons by working on the forces of nature. Over time, the performance of rites and sacrifices acquired in the minds of the Hindus a mystical power, a symbol of cosmic creation and recreation (Gokhale 1961, p. 96). Thus in later Vedic literature (*brāhmaṇas*) the cosmic law of *ṛta* was seen as being influenced by human will, which acted through performing sacrifices and rites (*karmakāṇḍa*) and could influence gods to do various things for human beings.

The mystical concept of *karma*, as manifested in the *brāhmaṇas* was developed into a philosophical concept by the Upaniṣadic thinkers. It was in the *Upaniṣads* that the concept of *karma*, in its association with ceremonial rites, was transformed and integrated with the emerging

Upaniṣadic theories of the relationship between the individual self and the cosmic self. The question that engaged the minds of Upaniṣadic thinkers was: If *ātman* represented continuity of self, was a manifestation of the cosmic self, what happens to it when one dies? What dies is the body and not the *ātman* — this was the answer they found. So the *ātman* is embodied from one life to another in order to perform *karmas*, and when it has performed its stock of *karmas*, the disembodied *ātman* merges with the cosmic self (or, as the idea was later developed in the *Purāṇas*, departs to a heavenly abode or to a hell if a residue of *karma* still remained as an indissoluble quantity). So the embodied selves are all different from one another. But the *ātmans* are not. The differences we observe in real life in terms of their behaviour, personality traits, degrees of misery and happiness they experience, are all due to the varying degrees of *karmas* they carry from their previous lives. This chain of *karma* is broken through right deeds and knowledge. When this happens, the self is freed from the *karmas* and attains salvation by merging itself with the cosmic self.

The *Chāndogya Upaniṣad* says: 'Just as he acts, just as he behaves, so will he be born' (III.14). The *Bṛhadāraṇyaka Upaniṣad* says: 'He who does good will be born good, he who does evil will be born evil, he becomes holy by holy deeds, evil by evil (III.2.13) . . . 'Therefore, in truth, it is said, Man is altogether and throughout composed of desire (*kāma*), in proportion to his desire is his direction (*kratu*), in proportion to his discretion he performs acts (karma)' (*Ibid*). The *Kaṭhopaniṣad* addressed itself to the question why different embodiments and manifestation of life take place. 'One goes into the womb of a mother, becoming incarnate in a bodily form; another enters into a plant. Each according to his deeds, according to his knowledge. So the *ātman* represents a continuity through births and rebirths until it burns all its accumulated *karmas* by good deeds and right knowledge and thus gets liberated from the cycle of birth and rebirth and attains the highest state' (V.7). The *Bṛhadāraṇyaka Upaniṣad* says: 'As a goldsmith taking a piece of gold forms another shape with it, makes it new and agreeable, so throwing off this body and obtaining that state of knowledge, the soul forms a shape which is more new and agreeably suited to the world' (IV.4.4; I.5.16; cf. also *Chāndogya Upaniṣad*: V.10.2). And, again: 'as a caterpillar which has wriggled to the top of a blade of grass draws itself over to a new blade, so does the man after he has put aside his body draw himself over to a new existence' (*Bṛhadāraṇyaka* IV.4.3; VI.2; *Chāndogya*, V.3.10).

Thus for the *Upaniṣadic* Hindus life is not for attaining worldly goals (though the *karmas* have to be performed by which the world keeps going) but for the transcendental goal of liberation of the soul. Each person is born to perform functions in whatever position he finds himself in order that the effects of his past *karmas* are undone. This means that he is born not to extract as best and as much as he can for his material existence, but to take only as much and in such quantities from the outside world as he needs for exhausting his past *karmas* while taking care not to create a new world of *karmas*. Thus the *Upaniṣadic* concept of *karma* served as a principle of individual morality which determined relationships between man and man, and man and nature. As such it was not applied to groups and statuses but to individuals as a sanction against an otherwise encroaching and unrestrained social behaviour. It implied a concept of individual responsibility for actions and its consequences, wherein right deed was its own reward and wrong deed its own punishment.

Since the significance of man's existence on earth lay in achieving the transcendental goal of *mokṣa*, worldly pursuits acquired meaning only in reference to this ultimate goal. Worldly pursuits were now guided by the explicitly defined principles of *dharma* and *karma*. The new concept of *karma* almost did away with the role of the Vedic gods and of the sacrificial rites to appease them for worldly prosperity, and that of the *dharma* with its possibility of such a temporal authority as the state emerging to enact laws and establish order. These functions were to be performed solely by the social organization itself by devising rules and codes based on the principles of *dharma* and *karma*.

Based on these principles, a new theory of social organization was developed in the *sūtras* and the *dharmaśāstras*, according to which the principle of *karma* determined man's status in society and that of *dharma* his duties as a member of a status group. But the *smṛtikāras* did not regard this as a break from the *Vedas*; on the contrary, they only sought to collate the remembered knowledge (*smṛti*) as it had come down to them. The *śruti*, which revealed *dharma* to man in the form of *vedas* thus began to be interpreted through the mediation of the *smṛtikāras* — the codifiers of the eternal rule of *dharma*. In this process, they developed a fully-fledged doctrine of *karma* which combined, on the one hand, the vedic concept of *ṛta*, associated with the sacrificial rites, and the *Upaniṣadic* concept of *karma*, associated with the doctrine of transmigration of souls and individual morality on the other. This led to a redefinition of the concept of *dharma* itself. *Dharma*, which was understood as a principle that maintained and even conditioned the cosmic order through the performance of sacrifices, began to be interpreted in terms of the emergent theory of *karma*, primarily, as a principle that maintains social order by assigning duties to *varṇas* and *jātis*.

The intellectual and ideological origins of the caste system probably lie in the emergence of the *karma* theory. It is a moot question of history whether the ideological change gave rise to the structure of castes, or whether the ideology was developed to justify the status system that was growing and being differentiated along with the rise of several new occupations. There is nothing unusual in history about transferring insights and categories developed through understanding the cosmic order to the understanding of the social order. What was unusual was the elaborate codification made from these principles and categories for the actual management of society by the *smṛtikāras*. What were poetic expressions, symbolic suggestions and mystical interpretations in the *Vedas*, the *brāhmaṇas* and the *Upaniṣads* about man's relationship with the cosmic order, or between the natural and the moral orders, were developed into cut and dried statements about *karma* and *dharma* for individuals and groups.

Thus from the Vedic concept of redemption from sin through sacrifice, to the Upaniṣadic concept of individual responsibility for acts on which depended one's salvation, to the *smṛtikāras'* concept of *dharma* as a set of rules for collectivities in which individuals were born according to their deeds in past lives, was indeed a long journey for the Hindus in search of external order and internal peace.

So powerful was the sway of the new theory of *karma* that not only did it transform the Hindu philosophy and social theory but Buddhism and Jainism also evolved their own versions of the *karma* theory. At the hands of the Hindu law-givers, however, *dharma*, which was once attached to an individual, became a collective attribute; a set of rules and duties to be followed by individuals born in statuses (*varṇadharma*), through different stages of life (*āśramadharma*) according to local customs (*deśadharma*) and needs of the time (*kāladharma*). It was even seen as a defining characteristic of an epoch (*yugadharma*). The concepts *karma* and *dharma* thus became integral to each other as acts and works carried out from past lives but ordered by statuses and stages of life. Thus with the help of the *karma* theory, evolved during the times of *brāhmaṇas* and *Upaniṣads*, *dharma*, the cosmic principle of the Vedas, became the principle of Hindu social organization elaborated in terms of duties ascribed by birth. Accordingly, those with good deeds in past lives were born to high statuses, and those with a stock of bad deeds were born into lower statuses. But within this broad generalization were incorporated several provisions for individuals to rise or fall from their given statuses, through performing good or bad deeds in this life, through possessing *guṇas* (qualities) and personality traits (*svabhāva*) appropriate to higher or lower statuses, and through knowledge and wisdom which could be acquired (and recognized as such) by a man or woman born to any status and even without direct or formal knowledge of the Vedas.

In the light of the above exposition the Western concepts of hierarchy and hereditary status system are clearly not adequate for a true understanding of the Hindu concepts of equality and inequality. In fact, in itself the concept of equality is irrelevant. In the perspective of the theories of *dharma* and *karma*, the social theories of Hindus appear *pro* order rather than anti-egalitarian. They emerge as theories orientated to maintaining order and harmony and open to modification and change according to the requirements of changing times. But this logic of Hindu social order, which equated justice with order and injustice with disorder, when worked out to its absurdest limits by the *smṛtikāras*, created a distinctive pathology in the social order, namely the system of 'untouchability'. In the following pages we shall explore the relationship of this pathology with the concepts of *dharma* and *karma* as they were developed by different schools of thought in the Indian tradition.

III

There is no dearth of literature on the Indian caste system which describes and critically examines its origin, nature, functions and role in contemporary times. In this *sūtra* and *smṛti* literature, by and large, the caste system has been viewed as an obstinately persistent, almost immutable, ideology and social order based on the principle of hereditary hierarchy and, in effect, of inequality, of which untouchability is the extreme manifestation. While it cannot be denied that the Hindu social order had developed its own pathologies, the point to inquire is whether the Hindu theory of social organization, based as it is on the principles of *dharma* and *karma*, views these pathologies as natural and justifiable functions that are integral to the working of the principles and the value system underlying them. Or are they viewed by the theory as undesirable consequences which can be separated from the principles and which, if eliminated, will not undermine the principles or affect their centrality for the ongoing social order? In my view, the durability of the caste order which has existed for centuries is not due to its structure, which in fact has changed considerably over time, but is attributable to the centrality that the principles of *dharma* and *karma* have retained in the world-view and value system of the Hindus, and consequently for their social order. In the remaining part of this paper my objective, therefore, is to examine the relationship between these principles and the changes in the structure as unfolded through the internal debate among the Hindu thinkers and law-givers — their own considerations and justifications for the order they propounded and upheld — and between them and the 'dissenters' who advanced counter-interpretations and counter-justifications for the principles and for their relationship with the structures. This process contributed to a continuous modification and change in the ideology and organization of the caste system and to its humanization.

The debate, carried on for centuries, covers a wide spectrum which includes such opposing traditions as the *Brahman* versus the *Śramana*, the *āstika* (believer in the authority of the Vedas) versus *nāstika*, the *brāhamaṇa* versus the kṣatriya, the spiritual versus the materialist schools of Lokāyata, the epic-Puranic literature versus the Jātakas. It is not possible here to do any measure of justice to the richness of the debate. We can only touch upon its main features relating to legitimation of the social order with the purpose of showing how the view of the caste system based on one chunk of literature, namely the *smṛtis*, is not only partial but woefully inadequate even for understanding the *smṛti* literature itself. The *smṛti* literature makes little sense if not placed in the context of challenges to which it constituted a response. Moreover, the *smṛti* view of the *dharma* and *karma* and the rules of inter-group relationships delineated by it cannot be held as solely representing the prevalent views and practices even of its times.

It is therefore necessary to locate the *smṛti* literature in the context of the overall debate on the principles and values and their relationships with the structures and practices. For reasons of convenience, we shall broadly characterize the debate as between the Brahminical and non-Brahminical traditions. It should be noted in this context that these were not mere intellectual debates, but they gave rise to, and sustained for long periods, revolutionary social and religious movements, ranging from Buddhism (in 600 BC) to bhakti (in AD 1200), which continuously modified and changed the social order for serving the needs of the changing times.

The Brahminic tradition

For the early Vedic Aryans the principle of the life world was only an imitation of the cosmic principle of the *ṛta*. *Ṛta* was the sovereign principle of the cosmos to which were subject the laws of nature, the will of gods and the fates of human beings. It is through rites, rituals and sacrifices that the *ṛta* was enacted by human beings to affirm their relatedness to gods (who were themselves governed by *ṛta* and hence *ṛtavrata*) and through them with the cosmos.

In the later Vedic period *ṛta* itself was conceived as a primordial ritual (cf. *Puruṣasūkta*) which creates and ordains the cosmos. By imitating and celebrating it in their day-to-day lives, through several daily and seasonal sacrificial rituals, human beings participate in the ongoing divine ritual and thus create and maintain their orders in the image of the divine order. Thus every household was enjoined to perform daily sacrificial rituals of *pākyajñas* to remind its members of their obligations to other human beings and creatures; and at the collective level, the various *śrauta* sacrifices were to be performed to mark the change in the economic cycle of seasons which reminded people that the worldly goods were gifts from gods and were meant to be shared collectively and enjoyed with discretion.

In *āgrāyaṇaiṣṭi*, a sacrificial ritual for reaping of new crops, it is enjoined that when men reap the fruits of earth, they must remember the bounty of gods. Similarly, in the rite of consecration of kings, the king is reminded that all authority proceeds from gods, and in the wedding rite the groom is told that the bride is given to him by Soma, Gandharva and Agni (RV.X.85, 41) and children and wealth are gifts of gods (*Ibid*, 41–4). Similarly, the individual's life cycle from conception and birth to death was punctuated by sacraments (*saṃskāras*), rites of initiation into new roles, specifying their social and religious obligations. Further, life was to be lived for goals that transcended the individual lifetime, for death was not an end of life, which in a different form extended beyond it (RV.X.14ff). The funeral rite therefore was the final rite for the body, but the rite of *śrāddha* was also to be performed for the departed soul. To be regulated in life (*vrata*) through rites and rituals was the supreme virtue, the *dharma*. It was necessary to ensure order not only in the lives of human beings but for attaining the goal that extended beyond life, the emancipation of the soul (*mokṣa*). In this sense the maintenance of religious and spiritual values was considered a primary function of the social order. Material pursuits were not rejected, but were sought to be regulated, limited and circumscribed for maintaining the primacy of the spiritual pursuits. By the time of the *brāhmaṇas*, the social order was thus cast essentially in terms of ritual order, whose function it was to regulate human thought and life sacramentally so that the social order remained eternally bound to the religious order.

Towards the end of the Vedic period, when kingdoms were established and Aryan speakers were settled in agriculture, the differentiation of classes in society became sharper and maintenance of the social ethic based on rituals became difficult to sustain. The supremacy of spiritual value was now sought to be maintained through establishing functional supremacy of a class that upheld ritual modes of life as superior to modes of life determined by the political or production functions. The relationships among classes began to be ordered in terms of a social hierarchy based on the degree of ritual practices each class followed and of the ritual purity it could maintain while performing such functions as engaging in wars or in various agricultural and other activities of production.

The purpose of the social order still was to maintain the salience of rituals, even as functions were becoming progressively differentiated in social, political and economic terms. Thus those who defined rituals and their significance, and, by presiding over them, acted as mediators between gods and men (the *brāhmaṇas*) were assigned a higher ritual status than those whose function it was to establish and maintain temporal power, albeit primarily to ensure maintenance of the ritual order. The functions of production (*vaiśyas*) and service (*śūdras*) however, were accorded respectively lower statuses in the ritual hierarchy, as these functions were considered unconducive to the spiritual pursuits and also affected the purity of the ritual performances. By this time a strict dichotomy of functions developed which pitted the spiritual against the material, the celestial against the temporal, the cerebral against the manual, with undoubted assertion of the former set of categories over the latter. This dichotomy, however, was sought to be theoretically ordered and harmonized rather than allowed to be developed in divergent and conflictual social tendencies, through a new concept of *varṇa* hierarchy, a hierarchy of classes based on the idea of hierarchy of values and functions, and, in practice, retaining the centrality of rituals and sacrifices separately for each class and for the social order as a whole.

Such a theory of *varṇa* order was for the first time articulated in the *Puruṣasūkta* in terms of its origin. According to *Puruṣasūkta* (RV.X.90) it is an order born of divine ritual, the sacrifice of the *Puruṣa*, the primordial Person who pervades the universe and exceeds it. It is the sacrifice of the Cosmic Person from which emerged four *varṇas*, each from His different limb: the *brahmaṇas* from the head, the *kṣatriyas* from the arms, the *vaiśyas* from the thighs and the *śūdras* from the feet. Like limbs of a body the social divisons (*varṇas*) are part of an organic whole and have been assigned different functions corresponding to the limbs from which they have emerged: spiritual authority (*brāhmaṇas*), temporal power (*kṣatriyas*), wealth (*vaiśyas*) and labour (*śūdras*). Again, like different parts of a man's body these functions were hierarchically ordered. The symbol of the body was thus devised to express the implicit hierarchy of values and goals in the functioning of the social order. Accordingly, the first two functions, the spiritual authority and temporal power, were instrumental in maintaining the spiritual values in the society through the maintenance of the ritual order. The other two, production and service, were held to be mere necessities and not values.

In brief, according to this theory or origin of the social order, the society was an organic unity born of a divine ritual, divided into four organically related but functionally hierarchical classes, whose primary function was to maintain the ritual orders in social life so that the primacy of the spiritual values is maintained over material pursuits.

With this theory of the divine origin of social classes, the hierarchy of functions, however, began to be articulated as a social hierarchy of classes. Although the justification of hierarchy was still in terms of the *dharma* — *dharma* as embodying such values as fairness, justice and truth — contentions about social superiority between *brāhmaṇas* and *kṣatriyas* also began to emerge. Even the spiritual authority (of the *brāhmaṇas*) began to express itself more and more in terms of ritual purity, and the temporal power (of the *kṣatriyas*) began to contend and even counteract Brahmanic claims of superiority. By mobilizing the laity (*vis*) directly as subjects, the *kṣatriyas* pressed the principle of *artha*, the polity (which later, in *arthaśāstra* and other tracts of *daṇḍaniti*, was to find full expression), as a primary principle without which, they held, even the *dharma* could not be maintained in the world. They also began to define the boundaries of the priestly role and thus questioned their claims of total spiritual authority.

While the *brāhmaṇas* and *kṣatriyas* were arguing among themselves about the importance of their respective functions in the society and thus claiming social superiority over each other, the fact of growing social differentiation of classes was generally accepted as part of the working of the principle of *dharma*. It was recognized that the society flourished with the growing differentiation and divisions of classes, but the principle which held it together as an organic social unity was that of natural justice or *dharma*. The *Bṛhadaraṇyaka Upaniṣad* (4.11–13), for example, thus describes the growth of social classes and the relationship between the social order and *dharma*:

> In the beginning this (the *Kṣatriya*) and other castes was indeed *Brāhmaṇa*, one only. Being one, He did not flourish. He projected an excellent form, the *Kṣatriya* — therefore, there is none higher than the *Kṣatriya*. Yet He did not flourish. He projected the *Vaiśya*. He did not still flourish. He projected the *Śūdra*. Yet he did not flourish. (Bṛhad. 4.14).

> 'So he created *Dharma*, the form of the good. *Dharma* is the ruler of the ruler. Therefore there is nothing higher than *Dharma*. So even the weak hopes [to match] the stronger one through *Dharma*, as one might through the King. (4.14). *Dharma* is the same as Truth. Hence when one speaks of the truth, he is said to speak what is right or just and speaking justly one is said to speak the truth. Both these — Truth and Justice — are the same (*Nirukta*, 6.26).

The Aryan society which was confined to the North of India and expanded later to the North-East began to be expanded southward in the early part of the post-Vedic period. This geographical expansion on the one hand and the growing social divisions, introduced through the emergence of new occupations and crafts on the other, posed a challenge to the continuation of the *varṇa* order as a fourfold functional division of the society. It became difficult to determine ritual statuses of several ethnic, occupational and social groups which crisscrossed the *varṇa* lines by following occupations that were traditionally not considered functions of the *varṇas*. Also, the vanquished local populations and the tribals on the peripheries of the social order could not be placed in the ritual hierarchy of the four *varṇas*. This posed a serious challenge to the *varṇa* order: how to maintain *varṇas* as a divine and perennial order and still accommodate in it the several ethnic, social and occupational groups that had now emerged and had acquired identities as specific *jātis*. Also, how to regulate the various particularisms of local and tribal populations and subject them to the rules of the wider order of the *varṇas*. A large part of *smṛti* literature is devoted to meeting this challenge to the *varṇa* order. The solution, it seems, was found in maintaining *varṇa* as a normative hierarchical order, a universal ideology and organization within which specific rules were devised for *jātis* (*jātis* were viewed as several autonomous local groups theoretically comprising the *varṇa* order, for whom the *dharma* was generally interpreted in terms of social convention, local practices, and behaviour by example and in terms of subjecthood of all *vis-à-vis* the King). All these criteria however, were sought to be justified as deriving their ultimate authority from the Vedas.

This, however, remained a tenuous solution. It became difficult to interpret *dharma* as an absolute principle governing all in an equal manner. It was now a principle *relative* to time and place and even to a status in the social hierarchy. While the principle of *varṇa* remained theoretically a measure of ritual status for broad classes, in practice *dharma* was interpreted in terms of *duties* attached to hereditary statuses. The functional division of classes based on the idea of *varṇa dharma* (functions of four classes) thus was now expanded to the division of the social order in several *jātis*, each with its prescribed *svadharma*. By the time of the post-Vedic period, the hierarchy of functions thus coagulated into hierarchy of hereditary statuses. Ritual ethnicity was extended to social ethnicity, and the idea of ritual purity to the practice of seclusion of groups following such occupations that involved ritually 'defiling' and 'unclean' activities like removing the carcasses, selling of liquor, officiating as or performing the role of a hangman, living primarily by performing funeral rites or by using clothes or other items discarded from the dead body and so on. Since occupations were generally carried out from father to son, occupations began to be associated with heredity. The hereditary occupational groups, usually sharing common ethnic characteristics, were identified as *jātis*.

With this development, the ritual disability of certain occupational-ethnic groups soon became their social disability. The ritually excluded population was now also socially and physically excluded and called *antyāvasāyin*, living on the peripheries, or on the cremation ground (Manu, 10.34–9), or *niravasita śūdra* (excluded and ritually defiled, and impurifiable as in Patañjali (*Mahābhāṣya*, Vol. II, p. 850). The *śūdras* no longer remained a general class but a collection of several *jātis*, classified into 'clean' and 'unclean', good and bad, high and low. In the *smṛtis* the unclean *śūdras* were enumerated by their *jāti* names: *Cāndāla, Mṛtapā, Paulakasa, Āndhra* and *Meda* as in the *Manusmṛti*. In the *Auśanasasamhitā*, *śūdras* are divided into *sacchūdra* (good *śūdras*) and *asacchūdra* (bad *śūdras*). The former are described as those who are entitled to perform certain rituals (like the *pakyajnas*) and are devoted in their service to the upper castes and the latter as those debarred from performing any Vedic rites and were for generations engaged in 'defiling' occupations (*Smṛti Sandarbha*, pp. 1548–9). Similarly the craftsmen (*śilpin*), were divided into skilled (*kalābhijna*) and ordinary. Bṛhaspati differentiates the crafsment (*śilpins*) from the manual labourers (*karmakāras*). Those who fashioned works from gold, thread, wood, stone and leather were the *śilpins* with their separate guilds and those who engaged in manual labour were the *karmakāras*. (*Bṛhaspatismṛti*, pp. 135, 142). The *Arthasāstra* divides the work-force, the *bhṛtakas*, into *uttama* (the higher ones), the *madhyama* (the middle ones), and the *adhamas* (the lower ones). Illustratively, the *Arthaśāstra* (Part I, pp. 117–18) mentions the soldier, the farmer and the potter respectively as belonging to these categories. With this growing subdivisions of class, especially among the *śūdras*, it became almost impossible to assign any ritual role or function to a set of *śūdra jātis* which engaged from generation to generation in occupations that were considered ritually impure. Since the fourfold *varṇa* order was defined in ritual terms these *jātis* began to be considered not belonging to the order or to a fifth order of the *Pancamas* of the *Antyajas*. They were considered not only as ritually impure *jātis*, but impurifiable and without remedy. This is how Patañjali (*op. cit.*) for example, defines the *Niravasita śūdra*, or *Auśanasa Samhitā* (*op. cit.*) describes the *asac-chūdras*, and Manu refers to their population by its *jāti* names and describes them as 'fallen' and impure. (Manu, 43. 44).

Similar divisions of *varṇas* into *jātis* took place among the *brāhmaṇas* and *kṣatriyas*. The *brāhmaṇas* who, for example, engaged in medicine or astrology were considered of lower ritual status. The *Daśabrāhmaṇa Jātaka* describes types of *brāhmaṇas* by the occupations they followed, such as wielding of arms, medicine, trade, agriculture and even services. Such occupational groups among the *brāhmaṇas* were regarded as of lower status than those who engaged in the learning of the Vedas and priestly functions.[4] Applying the *varṇa* criterion of hierarchy, in the *Śāntiparvan* of the *Mahābhārata* (III. pp. 2090–1) the *brāhmaṇas* following their original function of the learning of Vedas are called *brahmasamā* (the proper *brāhmaṇas*), those following the priestly functions, *devasamā* (akin to gods) and those following *kṣatriya* functions as aids of a king as *kṣatrasamā* (akin to *kṣatriyas*). Similarly it describes *brāhmaṇas* who in their occupation are akin to *vaiśyas* and to *śūdras*.

The *kṣatriyas*, like the *brāhmaṇas*, were also divided into *jātis* by occupations they followed. The *Arthasāstra*, for example, differentiates between those who were the rulers (kings) and those who were mercenary soliders or followed such occupations as agriculture and trade. (11.1). Similarly *vaiśyas* were divided into cowherds, farmers, traders etc. (p.10, 11, 32). Thus *jātis* emerged within each class and, in the case of those whose occupations digressed from the original functions assigned to the *varṇa* were considered ritually low or 'fallen' (*vrātyas*) from their original status. Manu (X.43, 44), for example, describes some such *kṣatriya* groups as *vrātya*, fallen by digression from their original functions. It also now became difficult to fit different *jātis* in the *varṇa* hierarchy. For example the status of a *brāhmaṇa* caste following the trade of agriculture could not be justified as 'higher' than a *kṣatriya* following his original function as a king and so on. Thus along with the fourfold vertical division of society into *varṇas* which were hierarchically ordered by their ritual status and practice of occupations in accordance with functions assigned to them in the Vedas, a continuous process of horizontal divisions of classes in numerous castes took place, creating considerable confusion about their social and ritual status within the all–India *varṇa* system, thus indicating regionalization of the hierarchical order. Very often different *smṛtikāras* assigned different *varṇa* statuses to the same caste; for example, while Patañjali Vol. II, p. 850) assigns the *Śakas* and the *Yavanas* the status of the *aniravasitaśūdra*, Manu (X.43, 44) calls them the *Vrātya kṣatriyas*, the lapsed *kṣatriyas*, who lost their original ritual status through social miscegenation.

An ingenious explanation was offered by the *smṛtikāras* for the growth of those numerous castes who followed occupations and lifestyles different from the ones enjoined on them in the scriptures. They regarded this change in the *varṇadharma* system as a definite degradation of the ritually oriented social order which could be prevented only by upholding ritual purity of the original *varṇa* functions. They persisted with the idea that pursuit of the crafts and occupations not sanctioned by the *varṇadharma* rendered these groups lower than those who performed the original functions assigned to the *varṇas*, and that this new order of *jātis* following occupations not sanctioned by the *varṇadharma* cannot be explained in terms of the divine origin. The origin of such *jātis* was therefore explained in terms of miscegenation of the four *varṇas* (*varṇasamkaratva*). The offsprings by the union between the male of the upper *varṇa* or caste and the female of the lower *varṇa* or caste (*anuloma*) were generally accorded the *varṇa* status of the father but considered somewhat lower than the offspring of the spouses belonging to the same *varṇa* (Manu. 10.6). But the offspring from the union between the female of the upper *varṇa* and male of the lower *varṇa* (*pratiloma*) were condemned to a low status. This explanation was used as a device theoretically in order to maintain the relationship of the *Jāti* order with the *varṇa* order which specified the relationship between occupational function and ritual status. Accordingly, several caste groups which transgressed the original *varṇa* functions as well as the indigenous tribes and tribes of foreign origin were listed in the *smṛtis* as miscegenated social groups with ritual disabilities attached to them. They were accorded a status much lower than those who maintained through generations the line of the original functions and of descent through marriages within the respective *varṇas* and by following occupations enjoined to them in the *Vedas*.

With the growth of several urban centres, in the post-Vedic period, the process of social and occupational differentiation became so rapid and the matrix of hierarchy so complex and fluid that the Brahminic tradition found it increasingly difficult to maintain criteria of ritual purity for the determination of social status of the numerous caste-occupation groups. Since the *varṇas* were by and large dissociated from the occupational functions, as a variety of occupations were followed by members of the same *varṇa*, the *varṇa* scheme remained only a theoretical reference for determining the ritual status of the *jātis*. In the empirical order of *jātis*, the ritual hierarchy was now sought to be determined by the degree of 'cleanliness' of an occupation followed by a *jāti* and by the line of descent it could maintain through permitted forms of marriages. But with the growing list of occupations and of ethnic groups that now came within the fold of the Hindu social order it became increasingly difficult to establish either a line of descent for a particular *jāti* or to unambiguously determine the ritual status of its occupation. This resulted in disputes about the ritual status of particular *jātis*. Some *jātis* who were once assigned higher ritual status by the earlier *smṛtikāras* were assigned lower status by the later ones and vice versa.

The *smṛtikāras* had now to devise a further explanation for this phenomenon of the upward and downward mobility of several *jātis*, which, in reality, might have taken place due to the change in a *jāti*'s occupation or in political power or through the practice of intermarriage with other castes. The *smṛtikāras* recognized such changes and even approved them eventually by conferring on a caste a ritual status appropriate to its changed social status. This was done through specifying rules of upward and downward mobility, the rules of *Jātyutkarṣa* and *Jātyapakarṣa* respectively. This was a kind of retrospective exercise to validate scripturally the changed statuses of castes so that the changes would be seen in accordance with the basic principle of ritual hierarchy of the *varṇas* and the rule to prevent social miscegenation could be made operative. Accordingly, detailed specifications are found as to how a caste through a continuous practice for generations of *anuloma* or *pratiloma* marriages of a certain kind can rise or fall in its status. For example Gautama mentions that the continued practices of *anuloma* or *pratiloma* marriages among the *varnas* or the *Jātis* for five to seven generations will result in a rise or a fall of the status of the progeny (1.4.11.99). While the change in the social status of a caste occurring through intermarriages (or through change in occupation or political power) is conceded, the progeny of the mixed marriages (*Varṇasaṅkaru* through *pratiloma* unions or even the progeny of *anuloma* marriage born through a *śūdra* woman is proscribed from performing the Vedic rites (ibid. 1.4.21). Manu, for example, clearly differentiates between the castes that have maintained their descent through marriages within the *varṇa*, whom he calls the *savarṇa jātis*, and the castes having a record of mixed marriages, whom he calls *anantara jātis*. He ascribes to the latter a status lower than the former (10.10; 10.14). Like Gautama, Manu also condemns the progeny of the *pratiloma* marriages and describes them as *bāhya* (the excluded) and *hīna* (the base) *jātis*. (10.28.31). Interestingly, Yājñavalkya, over and above the criterion of mixed marriages, also explicitly recognizes the fact of occupational change as leading to the rise or fall in the status of a caste. According to him the continued adoption of a profession of the lower caste by a higher caste will result in the fall of the status of that caste and vice versa (Yājñavalkya, pp. 25–7).

Thus Gautama, Baudhāyana, and later, in greater details, Manu, Uśanas and Yājñavalkya describe the occupations and the associated ritual disabilities of certain *Jātis*. This, they hold, occurred as a result of social miscegenation that took place through certain types of mixed marriages between the *varṇas*. For example the origin of the tanners' caste (*Karāvara* or *Carmakāra*) is traced through a certain line of mixed marriages by Manu (10.36). It is said to be descended from *Niṣāda* and *Vaidehī*. *Vaidehī* is a *pratiloma* progeny of *vaiśya* male and *brāhmaṇa* female and through successive intermarriages between *Vaidehīs* and *Niṣādas* arose the caste of tanners. Since the *Niṣādas* were the tribal hunters and *Vaidehīs* the degraded *vaiśyas*, Manu found an appropriate explanation for the ritually degraded status of the tanner. Similarly the origin of such other castes following the 'lowly' occupations as the *Sairindhras* (Manu 10.32) (trappers and hairdressers), the *Maitreys* and the *Kaivartas* (Manu 10.34) (the boatmen) is traced to their descent from *ayogva* women who wore clothes of the dead bodies and ate the left–over food of others (Manu 10.36). Several such castes have been listed by Manu, proscribing their occupations, and explicitly specifying their ritual and social disabilities arising from their 'unclean' occupations but justified in terms of their degradation due to social miscegenation (10.50; 10.51–6).

Some of the *śūdra* castes that were organized in guilds and had acquired economic importance, were, however, considered eligible for performing certain Vedic rites and thus formed a part of the *varṇa* scheme. They were accorded a place in civic affairs as they provided important sources of revenue to the King. But the wage–earners (*Bhṛtakas* as in the *Arthaśāstra*) and certain ethnic groups engaged in 'unclean' occupations (the *antyajas*, the *aniravasita śūdras*, the *antyavāsin*, and so on — the list of which became longer and longer with successive *smṛtikāras* — were treated as 'outcastes' having no ritual status whatsoever in the *varṇa* hierarchy, and as such were not entitled to spiritual emancipation. As we shall see later, the non-Brahminic movements from Buddhism to Bhakti contested this Brahminic position and asserted everyone's right, irrespective of caste, occupation or Vedic learning, to spiritual emancipation. They attacked centrality of rituals and emphasized individual's moral conduct and striving (*tapas*) as a means of spiritual emancipation.

The basic division of society by the time of the post–Gupta period was between the *savarṇas*, the castes that could be fitted in the ritual hierarchy of the *varṇa* order (the *brāhmaṇas*, the *kṣatriyas*, the *vaiśyas* and a section of the *śūdras*) on the one hand and the 'outcastes' on the other. Alberuni described this order thus: much, however, as these classes (the *savarṇas*) differ from each other they live together in the same towns and villages mixed together in the same house and holdings . . . . After the *śūdra* followed the *Antyajas* who render various services, who are not reckoned amongst any caste but are members of certain crafts and professions. They live on the peripheries of towns and villages. Below them are the lowest: 'the *Hadi*, *Doma*, *Candala* and *Badhatau*. They are not reckoned among any caste or guild. They are occupied with dirty work like cleaning of villages and other services.' They constituted 'one sole class and [are] distinguished only by their occupations. In fact they are considered like illegitimate children . . . The worst of all are the *Badhatau*, who not only devour the flesh of dead animals, but even of dogs and other beasts' (Sachau, *Alberuni's India*, Vol. I. p. 101).

With the decline in the power of the guilds the service castes and the castes of the craftsmen also fell in status and were condemned by Brahminical opinion as the *hīna jātis* or the lowly castes in the latter *smṛti* literature (cf. *Vīramitrodaya*).[5] With this, a growing number of the *śūdra* castes began to be pushed down to a servile status and were considered ritually ineligible for participating in several religious ceremonies of Vedic origin. One such important ceremony was the *upanayana saṃskāra*, a Vedic sacrament by which an individual was initiated to the learning of the Vedas. As Manu held, all individuals were born *śūdras*, and through the *saṃskaras* they became the *brāhmaṇas*, the *kṣatriyas* or the *vaiśyas*. In this sense, the *upanayana* was deemed a second birth for an individual by which he became the *dvija* or the twice born. But those born in the *śūdra varṇa*, as also the women, were not entitled to *upanayana* and thus debarred from the Vedic learning. A distinction thus arose, at one level, between the *dvijas*, the twice born (i.e. the *brāhmaṇas*, the *kṣatriyas* and the *vaiśyas*) on the one hand and the *śūdras* on the other. At another level, a sharp division took place between the *savarṇas* (i.e. members of all the four *varṇas*, including a section of the *śūdras* who were entitled to perform some Vedic rites, like the *Pākyajñas* (but not the *upanayana*) and the 'outcastes' who were held to be ritually 'impure' and 'impurifiable'. They were considered socially to be outside the ritual hierarchy of the *varṇa* order and theoretically to be the progeny of the most extreme and prohibited types of *pratiloma* marriages.

Thus in the period of rapid economic and social change which saw the emergence of several towns and cities and a great many new occupations, the Brahminic tradition stuck to the ritual criteria of social hierarchy, not allowing economic and political power to undermine the principle of *dharma* as was revealed in the Vedas. But, in the process of trying to reconcile the growing occupational and ethnic differentiations in society with the idea of the *varṇadharma*, the *dharma* that was once a cosmic principle, a law of nature, from which the values of truth and justice were derived to guide social relationships, was reduced to social conventions and ritual practices. What began as a process of integration and inclusion of many non-Aryan speaking ethnic groups in the *varṇa* system ended up as a process of exclusion of a vast population from the ritual order and consequently in fragmentation of the social order. Indeed, the original concept of *dharma* as a source of virtue and morality for all human beings survived, but only as a residual category of *sādhāraṇa dharma* — a set of rules to be followed by all irrespective of their *jāti* or *varṇa*.

Similarly, the concept of *karma* ceased to be the individualistic concept of the *Upaniṣads* which related an individual's action to its consequences. Instead, it served as a justification for one's birth in a *Jāti* or *varṇa* and for the privileges and disabilities attached to it. Further, by dissociating work from reward, as through the concept of *niṣkāma karma* in *Gītā*, it perpetually sought to keep the labouring population in a servile social status. Essentially, *dharma* came to be regarded as a set of rules, codified and explicated in the *smṛtis*, albeit on the authority of the *Vedas*, or of what survived of it in the 'memories' of the creators of the *smṛtis* (the *brāhmaṇas*), or in the example of the life led by the learned and the wise or in good practices which survived in the tradition (*sadācāra*). This changed concept of *dharma* thus served as a basis of social order, which positively linked *jātis* with occupations and heredity with ritual status and negatively sought to prevent social miscegenation. The Brahminic tradition thus persisted with the criteria of social evaluation which emphasized the ritual factor over the economic, and in effect despised all manual labour, with the result that several caste–occupation groups were condemned to a servile status, thus weakening the productive processes in the society. The Brahminic tradition was in fact engaged in an ideological battle to prevent secularization of the social order so that *dharma* continued to be its governing principle. This was sought to be done in the changed socio–economic context in which the principles of *artha* and *kāma* had begun to acquire, in reality, a much greater salience as elements guiding motivations and behaviour of many people.

The *smṛtikāras* were conscious of the difficulties involved in such an endeavour. They saw this period of change, as Āpastamba characterized it, as the age of 'transgressions' in which no 'Vedic' kind of 'seer' can be born (Āpastamba, 1.25.4.6) and in which one had to make do with the 'remembered' knowledge of the Vedas. In such a situation they saw their task in terms of laying down such rules and regulations as were necessary to minimize 'transgressions' and maintain the principle of *dharma* as a guiding force of the social order.

The non–brahminic tradition

In terms of its philosophical origins the non-Brahminic tradition is as old as, probably older than, the Brahminic tradition. (Pandit Sukk-hlaji, 1957, p. 119). The divide between the *brāhmaṇa* and *śramaṇa* traditions goes as far back as the early Vedic times and their relationship was considered as antagonistic as the one between a serpent and a mongoose (Patañjali, Mahābhaṣya, 2.4.9). But the philosophical differences became socially relevant some time during the later Vedic period with the emergence of the Buddhist Jain movements. By this time the *brāhmaṇas* had become a hereditary class and as such had begun to assert their social superiority over others. This was resented by the *kṣatriyas*, especially of the kingdoms and *janapadas* of the North-East, and also by the *vaiśyas* who had emerged from the submerged laity engaged in petty transactions and agriculture to become an economically and socially prominent class, constituting powerful guilds or *mahājanas*. They owned huge caravans which plied from the North-West frontiers to the North-East, and carried out banking and export trade expanding across the seas to Mesopotamia. Descriptions of such an emergence of the *vaiśyas* are, for example, frequently found in the *Jātakas*, especially *Cullaka Setthy Jātaka* (Jātaka No. 4, Jātakas, Vol. I, 114–23) and the *Bavaru Jātaka* (Jātaka No. 339, Jātakas, III, 126ff.)

The non-Brahminic movements, however, with the possible exception of some materialistic (the Lokāyatas) and hedonistic (cārvākas) schools, by and large, did not reject *dharma* and *karma* as central concepts governing the social order and as the sources of values in society. Nor did they reject the idea of functional division of labour in society and a hierarchy of values in which spiritual enlightment was considered the highest pursuit. But they did not consider rites and rituals as necessary practices for spiritual attainment. This resulted, on the one hand, in their challenging the social superiority of the *brāhmaṇas* and the low ritual status of the *śūdras*, on the other.

In this tradition the social esteem of an individual was related not to the idea of ritual purity, but to the purity of heart and right conduct of one's past. Thus, by dissociating the spiritual from the ritual and by questioning heredity as a criterion for determining the social esteem of an individual, the non-Brahminic tradition sought to establish the principle of religious equality for all — irrespective of *jāti*, *śilpa* (occupation) *varṇa* or access to Vedic knowledge (*mantra*). Its primary concern was religous equality, rather than the social and economic equality among the occupational and *jāti* groups. The non-Brahminic movements did recognize the conventional status differences, but held that these had nothing at all to do with one's ability for spiritual attainments or the respect and esteem members of different groups could receive from others in society. Thus, in this tradition, occupation and heredity were rendered criteria irrelevant for determining the religious status of an individual or a group. Membership of an occupational or a *jāti* group, it held, was by social convention and not necessarily by heredity; for members of the same *jāti* were found to pursue different occupations, and people following the same occupation to belong to different *jātis*. For example, the *Jātakas* mention *brāhmaṇas* who follow such occupations as medicine, trade, agriculture, service and even manual labour, and kings and soldiers came from different *varṇas* and castes. For example, the *Mahābhārata* states that a good king is one who establishes order, irrespective of whether he is a *kṣatriya* or a *śūdra*. The upshot of the Buddhist and the Jaina movements was a serious challenge they posed to the hegemony of the *brāhmaṇas* as a class: their exclusivist claims to spritiual knowledge, their hereditary entitlement to spiritual pursuits and above all their monopoly of virtue as a hereditary class.

Since the Brahminic power lay in the role *brāhmaṇas* had assumed for themselves as the bearers of the ritual order and as the authoritative interpreters of the Vedas, it was natural for the Buddhist, the Jaina and the other non-Brahminic schools to question, first of all, the very basis of the religious and social status of the *brāhmaṇas*. They did this, on the one hand, by rejecting the role of rites, rituals and sacrifices in the attainment of spiritual enlightenment, and, on the other, by rejecting the authority of the *Vedas* as the source of *dharma*. In the process, they defined *dharma* in terms of universal moral ideas such as truth and non-violence, self-control and charity and not an inherited virtue of a *jāti* or *varṇa*. It was a characterstic manifest in the right conduct of an individual and not a property of particular social groups. Similarly, *karma* was conceived as a series of actions and experiences emanating from desire and having consequences for an individual's life, for his or her suffering or happiness; rather than as a determinant of one's birth in a *jāti* or *varṇa* — thus contradicting the correlation of occupations with *jāti* and birth or descent with virtue. Thus, in this tradition, an individual belonging to any *jāti* or *varṇa* was considered capable of spiritual emancipation only if he understood the connection between his desire and his misery and strived through right conduct and *tapas* to overcome his 'desire' — *vāsanās*.

It is for this reason of holding spiritual emancipation as an ultimate goal of human life that the Buddha, for example, considered Brahmanhood as a quality to be aspired by all rather than a property of a particular class. In the *Sona Daṇḍ Sūtta*, the Buddha argues that Brahmanhood of a person is not determined by *varṇa*, *jāti* or *mantra* (knowledge of ritual codes). Brahmanhood depends, the Buddha argues, on one's character or *Śila* and intellectual prowess or *pānditiya*

(Dīgha I, pp. 104–5). In the *Assalāyan Sūtta*, when the *brāhmaṇa*, Assalayān, argues that the *brāhmaṇas* are the highest *varṇa* and that they, being born of the Supreme Being (*Brahman*), can alone be liberated, the Buddha clearly rejects the hereditary claim of the *brāhmaṇas* for spiritual emancipation. He argues that *varṇa* is not a natural or universal order for human beings. He points out that among the *yavanas* and the *kambojas*, as also in the other countries, the system of *varṇa* does not exist. Among the *kambojas* there are two classes, the freemen and the slaves, and the former can become the latter and vice versa. He further argues that all human beings are capable of inter-breeding (across *varṇas* and *jātis*), unlike members of two different species, and that therefore they belong to one species or one *jāti*, the human species. A *brāhmaṇa* woman conceives and produces children in the same way as the rest. Just as the fire produced from the sandal-wood and from ordinary wood is the same, the moral and spiritual attainments of persons of different *varṇas* are of equal importance. He then concludes that all human beings are entitled to and capable of emancipation (*Caturvarnim Siddhim*); for it can be achieved through *tapas* and is not dependent on *varṇa*, *jāti* or *mantra*. (Majjhima II, pp. 403, ff. pp. 462 ff.)

In the *Vasettha Sūtta*, when asked whether one becomes a *brāhmaṇa* by birth or by deeds, the Buddha again points out that by birth all are human beings and belong to one species. Birth only differentiates humans from other species; among themselves human beings can be differentiated not by birth but by the vocations they follow. A man may live by trade, tillage or service or by being a soldier or a priest; but all this does not qualify (or disqualify) him from becoming a *brāhmaṇa*. One does not become a *brāhmaṇa* or a non-*brāhmaṇa* by birth. It is by deeds that one becomes or ceases to be a *brāhmaṇa*. It is through austerity, chastity, self-restraint and control of senses that one becomes a *brāhmaṇa*. The importance of this argument of the Buddha is further increased by the fact that it recurs in *Majjhima* and *Suttanipāta* (Majjhima II. 1.C: Khuddaka, Vol. I, pp. 362 ff.).

In the *Sundarika-bharadvāja Sūtta* the Buddha implores: 'Do not ask about birth (*jāti*), ask about conduct (*mā jatiṃ pucchi cararanam ca puccha*), (Khuddaka I, pp. 334 ff). Thus the Buddha rejected birth, social position and traditional learning as measures of any one's esteem. What made a person respectable was his conduct and his pursuit of enlightenment. The *Vajrasūci* of Aśvaghoṣa unambigously declares: 'Brahmanhood is not [attained] by scriptures, or sacraments (*saṃskāras*), or birth or family or vedic learning or profession.

Brahmanhood is avoidance of sins' (quoted by G.C. Pande in *Śramaṇa Tradition*, p. 57). Similarly, in the Jaina texts Brahmanhood is dissociated from birth. The Jaina philosopher Prabhācandra, for example, argues that a *brāhmaṇa* cannot be distinguished from a non-*brāhmaṇa* as a cow from a buffalo, nor is there any way of showing purity of lineage. Brahmanhood is just a social description depending on social functions. There is only one human *jāti* which becomes many *varṇas* through functional difference (Vṛttibheda) (G.C. Pande, *Śramaṇa Tradition* p. 63). Thus in the non–Brahminic tradition while Brahmanhood was upheld as an ideal, a spiritual quality attainable by all, the hereditary class of *brāhmaṇas* was considered to be a social class as any other, with no particular inherited capacities for religious pursuits.

The Buddhist and the Jaina movements thus helped consolidation of the growing *kṣatriya* and *vaiśya* power, which challenged the Brahminic supremacy based on the idea of ritual hierarchy and the monopoly of spiritual enlightenment. It also entiteld the downtrodden castes to pursue spiritual enlightenment. Bodhisattva, for example, is frequently born as a *Cāṇḍāla*. The Jaina monk Haricsbala was a *Cāṇḍāla*. The Jainas even went to the extent of asserting that no spiritual leader (*arhanta*) or a monarch (*cakkavati*) or a powerful man (*baladeva*) could be born in a *brāhmaṇa* family because of its degraded lineage (*antakūla* or *tuccha*), poverty (*daridda*) or beggary (*bhikkhagu*) (Uttarādhạyayana, adhyāya XII).

The Buddhists and the Jainas thus rejected the latter Vedic and post–Vedic Brahminic principle of social superiority based on heredity, but accepted the superiority of spiritual and moral values over other pursuits. Spiritual and moral excellence, however, was considered attainable by all irrespective of *varṇa*, *jāti*, *śilpa* or *mantra*. They rejected all caste distinctions within their monastic orders. And in the wider society esteem was accorded by merit and excellence of individuals, not only in spiritual pursuits but, in practice, also in the art of ruling (without violence) and of creation of wealth. This made the ruling aristocracies of the *Rājanyas* and the *Sethīs* socially quite important.

The social impact of the Buddhist and Jaina movements, it seems, was largely in terms of expanding the elite class but had little long–term impact for the upward mobility of the *śudra* castes. While the new concept of *dharma* released the individual from the crippling notions of *varṇadharma* and *swadharma* of the *smṛtis* and entitled him to spiritual enlightenment, the concept of *karma* still remained dubious in the

Buddhist and Jaina tradition. However unwittingly, it bound the individual to the prevailing social reality of *jātis*. While the Buddhist and Jaina concept of *karma* held that the effect of the past *karma* was not divinely ordained and hence did not determine one's birth in *varṇa* or caste, it did connect the individual's present situation with his past actions and thus morally reconciled him to the social injustice of his present situation. According to this concept, an individual could transcend the effects of his past *karmas* through practicing certain virtues and acquiring a certain kind of knowledge. But this was more in the nature of psychic emancipation of an individual than social emancipation.

It was therefore possible, in the long run, for the Brahminic tradition to meet the challenge of the Buddhists and the Jainas by introducing certain concessions and modifications in the social order as Buddhism and Jainism did not constitute a fundamental challenge to the social order which gave primacy to spiritual goals over material pursuits. This process of accommodation and absorption of the critiques was sought to be achieved through the epics, *Purāṇas* and the neo-Vedantic literature, or the bhakti-cults.

Selected Bibliography

Sanskrit texts

Āpastamba Dharmasūtra, ed. A.C. Shastri and A.R. Shastri (Banaras, 1932).
Arthaśāstra, ed. and tr. R.P. Kangle, Bombay University, 3 vols.
Bṛhaspatismṛti, reconstructed by K.V.R. Aiyangar, G.O.S., (Baroda, 1941).
Gautama Dharmasūtra, ed. Anandaśrama, 1910.
Īśādidaśopaniṣadah with Sankara's Commentary, Kashi.
Mahābhārata, critical edition, B.O.R.I., Poona.
Mahābhārata, 4 vols., B.O.R.I., Poona.
Mahabhasya of Patañjali, ed. F. Kielhorn (Poona, 1962); *Mahabhasya*, (Rohtak, 1963).
Manusmṛti with the commentary of Kullūka, Chaukhamba Sanskrit Series (Varanasi, 1975).
Manusmṛti with the commentary of Medhātithi (Calcutta, 1932–9).
Manusmṛti, ed. V.N. Mandlik (Bombay, 1886).
Nirukta (Bombay, 1921), 2 vols.
Ṛgvedasamhitā with Sāyana's commentary, (Pune, 1933), 4 vols.
Ṛgvedasamhitā with commentaries, ed. Viswabandhu, (Hoshiarpur, 1965–6), 8 vols.
Yājñavalkyasmṛti (Bombay, 1914).

Other works

Apte, V.S., *The Practical Sanskrit English Dictionary*, 3rd edn. (Delhi: Motilal Banarasidas, 1965).
Aśvaghoṣa, *Vajrasūci*, Visvabhārati, 1960.
Bühler, G., tr., *Manava Dharmashastra*, S.B.E. XXV, (Oxford, 1886).
Fausboli, ed., *Jātakaṭṭha Vaṇṇanā*.
Gokhale, B.G., *Indian Thought through the Ages* (Bombay, 1961).
Kane, P.V., *History of Dharmaśastra* (HDS), 5 vols., B.O.R.I. (Poona, 1930–62).
McKenzie, John, *Hindu Ethics* (London, 1922).
F. Max Muller, tr., *The Upaniṣadas*, S.B.E. 1 (Oxford, 1879).
Lingat, Robert, *The Classical Law of India*, 1973.
Pande, G.C., *Foundations of Indian Culture*, vols. I and II (New Delhi, 1984).
Pande, G.C., *Śramanism and its Impact on Indian Culture*, L.D. Institute, Ahmedabad.
Radhakrishnan, S. and Moore, C., *A Sourcebook of Indian Philosophy* (Princeton, 1957).
Sachau, E.C., *Alberuni's India*, vol. I (London, 1910).
Sukhlaji, *Darsana aur Cintana* (in Hindi) (Ahmedabad, 1957).
The Thirteen Principal Upanishads, tr. R.E. Hume (Oxford, 1921).

3 Equality and Inequality in the Religious and Cultural Traditions of Hinduism and Buddhism*

Nirmala S. Salgado

Introduction

The central philosophical concept of the West . . . is *rational understanding* by which I mean intellectual mastery of the world around man, of the social structures in which he lives and of man himself conceived as a striving individual confronting both world and society . . . were we to state the characteristic perspective of the East in terms of this idea it would at once appear that, while its thinkers also prize man's rational powers, the primary purpose which they are expected to fill is that of guiding his quest for spiritual perfection that is his true destiny and which lies beyond reason.[1]

It would be inappropriate to disregard the value of religion in the major schools of Indian philosophy because these philosophies ultimately indicate an ultimate goal of salvation. Hence the relevance of understanding the concept of equality in India within the framework of religious ideology cannot be underestimated. Moreover the Western philosophical traditions, as mentioned, are primarily concerned with the position of man confronting the world that immediately surrounds him. In Indian thought human perception of the world is a manifestation of *māya*, and is only a part of a much larger cosmic whole.

Modern concepts such as liberty, equality, justice and freedom, which are necessarily interrelated and focus on the idea of the individual person, his position within a given state or society and his interaction with other individuals, had their roots in Greek tradition and were later nurtured in the West. In the religio-philosophical traditions of India, the idea of the individual person is distinct from

* I would like to thank Prof. Ratna Handurukande for the help she has given me in translations of original Pali and Sanskrit texts and for her comments. I am also grateful to Prof. Lily de Silva for her advice, and to Prof. A. S. Kulasuriya for the guidance he has given me throughout.

that in the West, not only because the individual's intuitive capacity is usually considered to be of greater value than rational power, which it both encompasses and surpasses, but also because of the different locus of the individual *vis-à-vis* his world.[2]

'The expression "human rights" is of recent origin. Even the French inspired *"droits de l'homme"* only goes back to the last decades of the 18th century.'[3] In all major religious traditions, the emphasis is less on rights in a society and more on duties by that society. Duty indirectly implies the rights of another, and hence it is necessary to ascertain what criterion determines a person's duty or another's rights, and how far this criterion is compatible with the universalist concepts that are being considered.

This paper is predominantly concerned with an investigation of selected texts. Modern concepts of equality are highlighted, but the hermeneutical approach has been followed as I have considered this to be a prerequisite for the preservation of the integrity of the texts. The texts that are examined here are from the main North Indian Hindu and Buddhist traditions. The principal sources that have been looked at are the Vedas, the *Upaniṣads*, the *Bhagavad-gītā*, the *Mahābhārata*, the *Dharmaśāstras* and certain Buddhist texts. Wherever possible I have given dates, but they are not to be taken as conclusive, for there is much disagreement amongst scholars concerning their accuracy. Dates, when mentioned, are intended to be indicators of trends and are there to help us observe the evolution of concepts and place them in their context. In this paper it has been important to identify the thought process that led to changing ideas, and examine not only the content but also the context and usage of the texts. This becomes especially significant when considering that the same texts had different ritual purposes at different times, and also when considering that these texts co-existed despite the appearance of the new schools of thought that may have provided a challenge to their authority. Thus this paper has tried to preserve the texts within the historical framework in which they arose.

It appears to be the case that in India the individual's social position is often determined by, or acts as a corollary to, his position in religion. This is probably because of the strongly religious basis of society which seems to be evident in most schools of thought. In examining attitudes to theories of equality in the religious and cultural traditions of Hinduism and Buddhism it will be noted that differences of order (*vaṃa*) or caste (*jāti*), gender, race and religion form the basis from which egalitarian theories may be perceived. Here we are concerned with an examination of North Indian religious and cultural traditions in particular, seen in the light of human rights concept of 'equality'. Equality or inequality may take several forms depending on status or power given to economic, political or social position. it is important to perceive that equality, as seen in a religious context, needs to account not only for the individual's position in everyday lay life, but also for the equal or unequal potential of any human being for salvation and his access to a share in the purely spiritual or religious life. With the religious tradition with which we are concerned in this paper, the two main differences of order/caste and gender are the ones which are considered throughout; the differences of race and religion are secondary, sometimes they are seen as *varṇa* differences and sometimes they are not referred to as being significant.

In the religious traditions in question, it will be noticed that one ideal or concept it usually considered to be the most important one and is responsible for the maintenance of a socio-religious equilibrium (for example, *ṛta, dharma*), or a single goal of a particular tradition is considered to exemplify ultimate perfection (for example, Brahman-hood, Buddhahood). In helping to maintain the ideal or attempting to realize the supreme goal, there may be certain barriers which are imposed on a specific category of people, and these barriers could be used as indicators of inequality in that tradition. Where there are no barriers, we may say that equality prevails. The main objective of this paper is to establish the criteria by which equality may be determined, and to investigate if and why individuals or groups of individuals are prevented from an access to benefits in this life or the hereafter.

The criteria of interpreting equality and inequality are highly theoretical in some cases, especially as the material for our investigation has been drawn from written literary sources. However, the literature from the earliest periods of Indian history forms the only substantial and continuous body of evidence from which we can work, and even if it did have little relevance to reality at the time of its creation, it probably had considerable influence later in moulding the minds and attitudes of the cultured savants, who in turn were respected as the ideal by members of their society.

From the Vedas to the Brāhmaṇas

The text which witnesses the earliest beliefs of the Aryan-speaking peoples in India is the *Ṛg Veda*. This text, which was composed over centuries before it reached its final form, remained within an oral tradition until it was committed to writing. It matters little when exactly it was written, or under what social circumstances, because the archaic language and verse forms show a certain uniformity which would have been almost impossible to alter at a later stage. There is little doubt, however, that the commentaries to this Veda, as well as the other Vedas, were composed at a later time.

Although the hymns were usually invocations to or made mention of deities, the deities were by no means the most important aspect of this early literature. The early Vedic texts were used for ritual or sacrificial purposes, and it is primarily from the usage of the texts that one may have some idea of the social structures of the time. The performance of ritual and sacrifice was considered indispensable for the maintenance of the cosmic order, *ṛta*. Ritual was performed both within and without the home and, originally, any householder could perform this.

We are told of the *Ṛg Veda*, that 'not only the older hymns, but the great majority of hymns give no evidence of class'.[4] The word *Brāhman*, which later denoted a class or order, here has no such significance, although it is used in the sense of *ṛshi* or of the creator of *brahma*,[5] where *brahma* meant the sacred power or word, necessary for the ritual. In hymns of liberality we have no mention of Brāhmans as recipients of gifts, as they were later considered, in the *Śatpatha Brāhmaṇa*.[6] Even in the later *maṇḍalas* of the *Ṛg Veda* we have indications that anyone could perform the necessary rites. Apart from the *Puruṣa Sūkta* and one or two other passages, we have no distinct reference to class, except when the Aryan *varṇa* is mentioned.[7] All householders had an equal opportunity to participate in the most important rituals. Thus we may say that in the realm of religion and within early Aryan-speaking, sacrificing society, there was no significant class distinction comparable to that which appeared in later Brahmanic texts.[8] However this egalitarian attitude does not seem to have extended to the peoples referred to as *Śūdras*, who appear in the later hymns of the *Ṛg Veda* and seem to mean the same as *dasyus* or *dāsas*. These peoples (if we do accept that they actually existed in reality and were not merely mythological characters), were considered to be 'non-sacrificing' and 'god hating'.[9] Indra is asked to 'slay those who offer no libations'[10] and 'the haters of devotion'.[11] From this we may infer that the sacrificers considered themselves superior to those of another faith, and wished to remain within their exclusive social unit. Thus the concepts of equality and respect for another people and culture were alien to them.

We have indications that married women performed certain rituals either with their husbands, or in place of them. This can be seen in the following hymns. In a hymn to Agni we are told: 'Nigh they approached, one minded with their spouses, kneeling to him adorable, paid worship.'[12] In a hymn to Indra, the wife is also acknowledged: 'Praiseworthy blessing hast thou laid upon the pair who with uplifted ladle serve thee, man and wife.'[13] 'Couples desirous of thine aid are storming thee, pouring presents forth to win a stall of kine . . .' We are told later that: 'O Gods, with constant draught of milk, husband and wife with one accord, press out and wash the Soma juice.'[14]

It is evident that the place of woman *vis-à-vis* sacrifice was seen in terms of her married status, and she is usually a companion or representative of her husband. We do not find reference in the *Ṛg Veda* proper (as opposed to its commentarial tradition) to unmarried women participating in sacrifices alone and in their own right. This would indicate that, unlike men, women had to be married to have a share in the religious performance.

In one hymn, the sacrificial altar is referred to as a woman, and one may infer that woman, as such, was not scorned: 'The youthful one, well shaped with four locks, braided, brightened with oil, puts on the ordinances.'[15]

The significance of the married woman, as mentioned, was seen in the light of the sacrificial ritual alone and did not have relevance to her mental capacity. We are told in later hymns that 'Indra himself hath said, the mind of woman, brooks not of discipline'. 'Her intellect hath little weight.'[16] 'With woman there can be no lasting friendship: hearts of hyenas are the hearts of women.'[17]

Yet the supreme importance of acknowledging the necessity to sacrifice seems to be a criterion that could give a devout woman more respect than an irreligious man: 'Yea, many a woman is more firm and better than the man who turns away from the Gods and offers not.'[18]

We may conclude from the text, that in early Ṛg Vedic society the position of the married woman was on a par with that of the householder within the sphere of the sacrifice and ritual.[19] Although there are indications that woman's mental capacity was then thought to be lacking, it is necessary to stress that this particular deficiency was not considered an obstruction to woman's participation in religious activity, and did not prevent the married woman from sacrificing. The position of the householder was exclusive to the sacrificing society, but was equal to that of any other householder, as far as religion was concerned.

The *Brāhmaṇas* and *Āraṇyakas*, which were composed after the early parts of the *Ṛg Veda*, are at times indistinguishable from each other. In the *Brāhmaṇas* we have evidence of a certain rigidity in the social structure, that was not apparent before. Now the Brahmin alone had the exclusive privilege of maintaining *ṛta*, and was considered a 'god upon earth', for he was considered to be the only category of human being who knew how to utter the sacred words effectively. The four main classes or orders, and rules concerning them, are mentioned, and seen in connection with certain ritual performance. Ideas of 'purity' and 'impurity' emerge in relation to correctly performed ritual, and now we find rules prohibiting exogamy, and also rules requiring the son to follow the father's occupation.

The social inflexibility can be seen reflected in the religious rites themselves, for the priesthood had become increasingly specialized. Priests in the later Vedic period had to devote themselves more to one sacrificial function, and would have to undergo training as invoker (*hotṛ*), singer (*udgātṛ*), or one responsible for ritual activity (*adhvaryu*), rather than be enabled to perform all three functions.[20] Looking at the *Brāhmaṇas*, we could say that the perfectly performed ritual was of greater importance than the purpose of its performance — the upholding of *ṛta*, and that what in earlier Vedic times was the means later became an end in itself. The slightest error in the ritual could mean disaster, and we have mention of the sacrifice running away from the Brahmins, who then needed to pursue it. We may say that the greater rigidity apparent in the texts, and the value of the ritual and the priests were probably developments that resulted from an Aryan-speaking society being threatened in a changing cultural milieu, and therefore wishing, probably, to reassert and fortify its position in a dynamic and expanding society. Here the maintenance of the socio-religious equilibrium in favour of the priesthood necessitated an inegalitarian attitude within society.

The place of woman in this period was considerably lower than before. She was now considered to be in the same category as the *śūdra*, the dog and the crow. However, we have no evidence confirming that widow burning was either practised or recommended by any of the *Brāhmaṇas*.[21] In the Brahmanic texts we may say that woman was considered inferior to man, and that she was impure in religious terms. She was recognized as necessary for the procreation of sons,

who, unlike daughters, were capable of and indispensable for performing funerary and other rites, which ensured the happy after-life of the
father and ancestors.[22] Winternitz has summarized the place of woman
in this later Vedic, or Brahmanic period well: '*Dass die Frau immer die
beste Freundin der Religion, die Religion aber keineswegs eine Freundin der
Frau gewesen ist, zeigt sich nirgends so deutlich wie in Brahminismus.*'[23]

The Upanishads

In the Upanishads, the earliest of which date back to 600 BC, just
before the rise of Buddhism, we see a new attitude to sacrificial ritual
and the priestly order. Here the correct ritual performance, together
with the Brahmins who perform it, are given a position that is
subordinate to knowledge of *Ātman/Brahman*, which is considered to
be of primary importance.[24] The knowledge of *Ātman/Brahman*,
together with the symbolism of the sacrificial ritual, may in this period
have replaced what was previously the most important element — the
sacrificial ritual itself. For both knowledge of *Ātman/Brahman* and
ritual performance were at different times the only paths leading to a
happy after-life. Knowledge of the Vedas is recognized, but given its
place. Thus the son who has studied all the Vedas is told by his father
that he has not learned all that is necessary.[25] Knowledge of the four
Vedas and their commentaries are a lower knowledge.[26]

In the immediately preceding Brahmanic period where ritualistic
performance was of supreme importance, we notice how certain
barriers to participation in this were imposed on specific categories of
person. In the Upanishads however, a new attitude to equality may be
perceived, for now barriers to the attainment of knowledge are
noticed which are not based on birth or social status but either on the
individual's own willingness and capacity for attaining knowledge or
on the pleasure of the gods.[27] Thus new norms of egalitarianism
appeared.

Though the equal potential of each individual to achieve the ultimate goal seems to be allowed, it is clear that the esoteric teachings
were highly secret and precious and could only be understood by a
selected group of individuals,[28] and that it was displeasing to the gods
that humans should know the self (*ātman*).[29]

It is probably in these texts that a desire for the birth of a daughter
was first expressed. However, there are some indications of a greater
respect given to males than to females. This may perhaps be more a

reflection of the Brahmanical society from which the Upanishads emerged rather than ideas intrinsic to the texts themselves. Thus Maitreyī, Yājnyavalkya's wife, who is a discourser on sacred knowledge, is contrasted with his other wife, Katyāyanī, who has 'just a woman's knowledge in that matter'.[30] The value of a son (as opposed to a daughter) appears on several occasions. We are told that 'He who knows this wind thus as a child of the quarters of heaven mourns not for a son.'[31] The son of Vājásrava is considered 'his whole possession',[32] and 'a father may teach this Brahman to his eldest son or to a worthy pupil but to no one else at all',[33] and the last wish of a dying father is to summon his son.[34]

A denial of distinction based on *varṇa* and gender is evident in the concept of the universality of all souls and the ultimate oneness of all elements. Thus we are told that 'not for the love of Brahmanhood is Brahmanhood dear, but for the love of the soul Brahmanhood is dear, Lo, verily, not for love of *Kshatrahood* is *Kshatrahood* dear, but for love of the soul *Kshatrahood* is dear'. Similarily: 'Lo verily, not for love of the husband is a husband dear, but for love of the soul (*ātman*) a husband is dear, Lo, verily not for love of the wife is a wife dear, but for love of the soul a wife is dear.'[35] We are also told that a failure to see the oneness of existence leads to reincarnation.[36]

The importance of the knowledge of symbols in the Upanishads cannot be overestimated, for it is through the symbol which represents the ultimate that one can attain salvation. The symbol, like the concept of selfhood, can be seen as transcending the domain of differentiation. Thus where the chant is the symbol, we are told that

> the Chant (*sāman*), verily, is speech. It is *sā* (she) and *ama* (he). That is the origin of the word *sāman*. Or because it is equal (*sama*) to a gnat, equal to a fly, equal to an elephant, equal to these three worlds, equal to this universe, therefore, indeed, it is the Sāma Veda. He obtains ultimate union with the Sāman.'[37]

Breath, which is an element common to all human beings, without discrimination, frequently occurs as a symbol of *ātman/Brahman*. Similarly food, which is common to all humans, is considered representative of the ultimate.[38] A symbol in the Upanishads by its very nature defies differences amongst them and lends itself to the support of equality.

From the foregoing we may conclude that there are basically two or three spheres in which attitudes to equality may be discerned. One is the universality of the knowledge *ātman/Brahman* itself, represented symbolically. Another is the individual's potential for the attainment of knowledge. There is, however, also a certain secrecy that must be preserved in the transmission of knowledge, which reveals an elitist attitude in the Upanishads that is found in other religions too. In no spheres are there barriers to a person's attainment of the ultimate because of their status or gender by birth, and we may say that equality has a new significance that was not recognized in previous texts.

The Buddhist Period[39]

It appears to be the case that scholars, when considering the early Buddhist period, usually either completely ignore or lightly dismiss the value of the Upanishads. It is possible that parts of most of the thirteen principal Upanishads were created before the Buddha's time, and, according to Winternitz, only the *Maitri* and the *Māṇḍūkya* Upanishads were probably post-Buddhist.[40] Despite the roughly contemporaneous thoughts found in Upanishadic and Pali Buddhist texts, it is perhaps noteworthy that the Buddhist texts provide us with considerably more material than the Upanishads criticizing the Brahmanical social structure. Yet the attitude to this structure appears to be similar in both texts.

A myth of the origin of kingship is recounted as follows in connection with the evolution of society.[41] Originally sexless beings made of mind existed peacefully. As time passed, the savoury earth manifested itself. The beings tasted it, and craving entered into them. From that time onwards, sex differentiation, private property, greed, selfishness and lying developed, and all beings decided together to choose one who was 'the handsomest, the best favoured, the most attractive' who would be 'wrathful when indignation is right . . . who would banish him who needs to be banished', and he, being democratically chosen, was called the *Mahā Sammata* or *Khattiya* or *Rāja*, who charms others by the *Norm* (*dhamma*).[42]

It is evident from this that the principle of moral righteousness and social security was the criterion which determined justice to all individuals on an equal basis and was the primary factor that necessitated and defined the function of a king. The human species as well as the theory of kingship were products of a process of moral degeneration. Birth was of no consequence in either justifying kingship or meting out punishment. It was also considered the duty of the

Buddhist state to ensure that there was no crime, for we are told that 'the state should adopt means for the acquisition of wealth on the part of those devoid of wealth'.[43]

The Buddha considered that righteousness was something which could ideally be found in every individual, regardless of his birth or social status, and that this was the main factor indicating a person's spiritual potentiality. Therefore, theoretically every human being could attain the ultimate goal of nirvana. Reference to and recognition of *varṇa* and *jāti* in Buddhist texts was seen in purely mental, spiritual terms of behaviour, and not in the traditionally accepted form. Thus the characteristic mark of a *Brāhmaṇa*, as described by the Dhammapada, is that he is not necessarily recognizable to the external eye, and this particular quality is to be found in every verse of the '*Brāhmaṇa Vagga*' of the *Dhammapada*, and indicates that any righteous human is a potential *Brāhmaṇa*. We are told that: 'Not by matted hair, nor by family, nor by birth does one become a *Brāhmaṇa*, but in whom there exist both truth and righteousness, pure is he, a *Brāhmaṇa* is he'.[44]

According to the *Vasetthasutta*, mankind is said to belong to one biological species (*jāti*), and although living creatures can be distinguished according to biological differentiation, mankind cannot be thus differentiated. The biological equality of mankind may indicate a respect in Buddhism for all races, and to a certain extent for all religions too.

> I will explain to you — O Vāsettha, in due order the exact distinction in living beings according to species (*jāti*), for their species are manifold.
> Know ye the grains and the trees although they do not exhibit (it) the marks that constitute species are for them and (their) species are manifold.

He continues to describe the various categories of living organism which could be differentiated, for they constitute different species (*jāti*) including worms and moths, four-footed animals, serpents, fishes and birds, and finally he comes to man.

> As to those (aforementioned) species, the marks that constitute the species are abundant, so in men, the marks that constitute species are not abundant.
> Difference there is in beings endowed with bodies but amongst men, this is not the case, the difference amongst men is nominal only.[45]

Moreover, we have passages confirming the denial of hereditary differentiation, for we are told that: 'Not by birth does one become an outcaste, not by birth does one become a Brahman, by deeds one becomes an outcaste, by deeds one becomes a Brahman.'[46]

There are recurrent examples of the non-recognition of the existing caste order in Buddhist literature[47] and this aspect is clearly shown in the story of Ānanda and the *Chandāla* maid.[48] Ānanda accepts water from her, demonstrating the irrelevance of class or caste for him, despite her protestations. Eventually this so-called low-caste *Chandāla* maiden is admitted into the order of Bhikkunis, much to the disgust of the nobility of Srāvasti. They even go to discuss this incident with the Buddha as it is an important matter of prestige for them. It is not until after their discussion with the Buddha that they are convinced of the unimportance of social birth. We are told that admission to the order is open to all castes and that names were changed on entrance as these are otherwise an indication of status by birth.

The social role of woman in early Buddhism is usually seen in terms of her function within the household as wife and mother. She is generally not seen as an individual entity without the household, although we come across exceptional cases. In the following passage the Buddha is trying to comfort King pasenadi of Kosala, who has just heard of the birth of a daughter:

> A woman child, O lord of men, may prove,
> Even a better offspring than a male.
> For she may grow up wise and virtuous,
> Her husband's mother reverencing true wife.
> The child she may bear may do great deeds,
> And rule great realms, yea, such a son,
> Of noble wife becomes his country's guide.[49]

Here the newly born daughter is seen in the future as a good wife, and the mother of a son. Her son, however, is seen as an individual who may have a valuable contribution to make to his country.

In another passage, where the Buddha gives advice to young girls, we see once again how their place in society, though respected and recognized as worthy, remains within the household.

> Therefore girls, train yourselves thus: To whatever husbands our parents shall give us, for him we will rise up early, be the last to retire, be willing workers, order all things sweetly and affectionately. Train yourselves thus girls . . .
> And in this way too girls: Whatever our husbands' households consist of, servants and messengers and work people, we will know the work of each one of them by what has been done . . . we will portion out the soft food

and the solid food to each other according to his share. Train yourselves thus girls.[50]

The next passage confirms that, in early Buddhist India, women as a rule did not hold certain positions in public. It also reveals a different attitude to women in Buddhism. That Ānanda should query the Buddha on this subject shows that the question of woman's place in society then did arise. 'Pray Lord, what is the reason, what is the cause why women neither sit in a court[of justice] (*sabhā*) nor embark on business (*kammanta*), nor reach the essence of the deed? (*kammojan*).' The Buddha replies: 'Womenfolk are uncontrolled, (*kodhano*) Ānanda, womenfolk are envious (*issukī*) Ānanda, womenfolk are greedy (*macchari*) Ānanda, womenfolk are weak in wisdom (*duppañño*) Ānanda. That is the reason, that is the cause why womenfolk do not sit in a court of justice, do not embark on business, do not reach the essence of the deed.'[51]

We have, on the other hand, several examples of women gaining spiritual insight, and it would appear to be the case in early Buddhism that gender was no obstacle to the exceptional woman who could realize her full spiritual potential.[52] Thus Khujjuttārā attained stream–entry on hearing the Buddha's discourse, Sāmāvati eventually attained arahantship, and Pāṭācārā, who attained complete emancipation, was rewarded with the title of the 'Keeper of the Vinaya' amongst nuns. When King Pasenadi questioned the nun Khemā on the existence of an Awakened One after death and, on another occasion, asked Queen Mallika if she loved anyone more than herself, he received replies from them which corresponded almost exactly to what the Buddha would have said in their position. According to later texts, females are denied the possibility of attaining the ultimate perfection of Buddhahood and the higher stage of Bodhisattvahood (one that is incapable of sliding back). In the following passage, Sāriputra speaks to the daughter of the Nāga King:

> It may happen, sister, that a woman displays an unflagging energy, performs good works for many thousands of Aeons, and fulfils the six perfect virtues (*Pāramitās*) but as yet, there is no example of her having reached Buddhaship, and that because a woman cannot occupy the five ranks, viz. (1) the rank of Brahma (2) the rank of Indra (3) the rank of chief guardians of the four quarters (4) the rank of Cakravartin (5) the rank of a Bodhisattva incapable of sliding back (*avaivartika*).[53]

The princess then gave away a gem, showing her indifference to worldly possessions, and then, almost immediately, 'the female sex of the daughter of Sāgara the Nāga King, disappeared; the male sex appeared and she manifested herself as a Bodhisattva'.

In another passage we are told that, 'should a female . . . after hearing this Dhamma parayāya grasp and keep it, then this existence will be her last existence as a woman . . . will . . . be (re)born in the world of Sukhāvatī . . . There will he (who formerly was a female) appear seated on a throne consisting of a lotus.'[54]

The Buddha showed much hesitation in first allowing the initiation of nuns. He refused his aunt Mahāpajāpati Gotami thrice when she made the request to start an order of nuns, and only considered her request after listening to Ānanda and after Mahāpajāpah Gotamī's acceptance of the eight *Garu Dhammas*. On this occasion, the Buddha is recorded as having considered it possible for a woman to realize the fruit of Entering-the-stream, and of Once-Returner, Non-Returner and Arhantship. The behavior of Ānanda in favouring women's entrance into the order was later seen as a fault, which was held against him. The Buddha eventually accepted the entrance of women into the order, saying that 'If woman had not received the going forth in the doctrine, and the discipline, the religious system and *brahmachariyā* would have lasted longer — the good doctrine would have lasted for a thousand years, but as women have gone forth now, Ānanda, the good doctrine will last only 500 years.'[55]

The Buddha allowed women to enter the order on the condition that they accepted eight rules. These rules ensured that almswomen were dependent on almsmen for most ceremonies, and that they could not, therefore, within the *Sangha* be considered as being equal to the latter. We are told that an almswoman even of a hundred years standing must bow down to an almsman, even if only just initiated; almswomen were not to spend the rainy seasons where there was no almsman, and the official admonition of almsmen by almswomen was forbidden, but not vice versa.[56]

It is evident that, in early Buddhism, the social role of woman was in keeping with the times. She was generally honoured though restricted to the household life,[57] and her spiritual potentiality was not always denied. In later Buddhism, however, it is apparent that the female is not deemed to have as great a spiritual capacity as the male. We may say that, in Buddhist society, girls and young women were envisaged as future mothers and wives. Women obtained the ordination with some difficulty, unlike men.

The main difference of persons in Buddhism, therefore, is not based on that of order or caste, but on that of gender. This does not imply that inequality between man and woman in lay life was intended. However, it does indicate that the Buddha may have considered the lay life as more appropriate to women than the religious life, and also that the ideal Buddhist man was always closer to Buddhahood than the ideal Buddhist woman.

Bhagavad-gītā

The *Bhagavad-gītā*, which was composed about 200 BC, is said to have reached its present form in about the second century AD.[58] Examination of this text is vital, as it may be considered a model of Indian culture. It is also the first text which mentions the way of *bhakti*, which is the main form of worship among Hindus today. This text, though appearing in an epic context, is primarily a religious text, for it attempts to point the way to salvation.

The significance of equality here can be seen primarily in relation to one's duty by one's *vaṃa*, which may be equated to one's duty by God. Thus one may say that a certain inequality is introduced where birth into a specific caste determines one's lifetime's duty by that *vaṃa*. One's access to the most important goal of salvation, however, is not, unlike in some texts, at all conditional on class or gender.[59] but it is particularly dependant on one's attitude to one's class. Arjuna, whose *dharma* as a *kshatriya* demands that he fights and kills his cousins and uncles, hesitates on the battle field. His own moral consciousness is disturbed and he cannot fight to kill those of the same blood. Krishna, the god, friend, cousin and charioteer, however, insists that Arjuna is asserting his own self and ego by refusing to behave as is appropriate to one of the warrior caste. He indicates that by succumbing to his own feelings, Arjuna would be asserting his own ego, and ignoring the ultimate unity of all beings, or *ātman*, which in all beings is the same, and that Arjuna is acting with the fruits of his deeds in mind.

The totality of all souls may be seen, for our purposes, in terms of equality of all souls and all beings, although this totality is absolute and transcends the domain of equality and inequality because of its metaphysical character. By considering the fruits of his work and not acting as a warrior should, Arjuna would be acting out of accordance with *karma yoga*, or the way of work, which is one of the main paths that leads to *mokṣa*. Thus duty in action, which can be adhered to by a correct understanding of Krishna's exposition, is of prime importance. The concept of rights here is secondary and subordinate to that of duty, for Arjuna is told that 'to action alone hast thou a right and never at all to its fruits; let not the fruits of action be thy motive; neither let there be in thee any attachment to inaction'.[60]

As seen earlier, action has been determined by one's *varṇa* and by birth, but a common attitude to one's *varṇa* action is ideally required for all individuals, irrespective of their particular *varṇa*. Taking this into account one may say that the criterion (of *mokṣa*) by which a theory of equality can be determined maintains a certain egalitarian equilibrium, whilst at the same time acknowledging the validity of the different *varṇas*. Thus equality remains partially valid in the purely religious sphere, but *varṇa* differentiation exists in lay life.

Apart from and in addition to *mokṣa*, the concept of equality is prominent in religo-philosophical ideas concerning living creatures in general. Thus we are told that

> Sages see with an equal eye, a learned and humble Brahmin, a cow, an elephant or even a dog or an outcaste.
> Even here (on earth) the created (world) is overcome by those whose mind is established in equality. God is flawless and the same in all. Therefore are these (persons) established in God.[61]

Later Krishna says that 'He who is equal-minded among friends, companions and foes, among those who are neutral and impartial, among those who are hateful and related, among saints and sinners, he excels.'[62]

The new religious feature of *bhakti*, which appears for the first time in the *Bhagavad-gītā*, is one that again denies any social or religious barriers to one's attainment of salvation. This new form of worship is unconditional. It appears that of the three paths of salvation, the path of *bhakti* is the easiest, and it is also the one open to the greatest majority of worshippers. However, of the three main paths of salvation, none is necessarily superior to another, and they are different only to suit the needs of the different persons involved. In these three forms of worship, the most significant and common phenomenon is the attitude of the individual to God, which need not be any one god in particular. Thus we see an equal opportunity for all humans to approach God: 'Even those who are devotees of other gods, worship them with faith, they also sacrifice to me (Krishna) alone, O Son of Kuntī (Arjuna), though not according to the true law.'[63]

Bhakti is seen in a twofold capacity in the *Gītā*. It is the devotion of the *bhakta* to God and also, as mentioned earlier, unconditional love or grace of God to a specific devotee. Here one might see a certain partiality or inequality as far as the love of God is concerned. There appears to be no special reason for God to love any particular individual. Thus we notice how the transcendental nature of God defies to a certain extent our attempt at interpreting equality and inequality in religious terms; yet God's love is that which determines the after life of the individual. Thus Yudhīshthira, who is the son of *dharma* incarnate, and yearns to understand the nature of God, is not the privileged one who is granted the manifestation of Lord Krishna. However Arjuna, his brother, who hesistates before carrying out his *dharma* before Krishna, by refusing to fight, and who appears rather foolish (he is given a lengthy explanation of the nature of God and worship in the *Gītā* but forgets this shortly afterwards), is the lucky one who is allowed to see with a Divine Eye the true form of Lord Krishna, which is something that 'even the Gods are ever eager to see'.[64]

The *Gītā* is a text that acknowledges differences based on functions in life and also on the religious quality (*guṇa*) of humans. However these differences themselves are not the main obstacles to religious salvation. The ambiguity of the text itself, which we may come to terms with through the unique nature of God, does not allow us to interpret this text in strictly egalitarian terms. So we may say that from the purely religious point of view clearly distinguishable theories of equality cannot be extracted from this text, although functional differences in terms of *varṇa* are recognized and do apply to the lay person.

The Mahābhārata

When examining this text, it is necessary to remember that we are considering a depiction of ideals and values which might not have had great relevance to society at the time of its composition, but which probably did represent models which were recognized and admired in later centuries.

Throughout the text we notice a certain validity and importance given to hereditary *varṇa* status. These can be discerned as being responsible for particular characteristics of an individual, whether he realizes that he belongs to a specific order or not. We have such an example in the case of Radheya (Karna) who is the half–brother of the

Pāndavas, and is born to a *kshatriya* mother and discarded. He believes he is the son of a *sūta*, or chariot driver, considering his adopted parents as his true parents. However, as he grows up, he displays *kshatriya* peculiarities, he has an inexplicable desire to become an archer rather than drive a chariot, as his alleged father does.[64] Later, he sets out from home in order to learn archery, but has great difficulties in finding a teacher, for he claims to be the son of a *sūta*, and because of his supposedly low birth is refused lessons and despised. Eventually, pretending to be a Brahmin, he obtains a teacher. However, one day, his Kṣatriyahood is revealed to the teacher, for when the latter is resting on Radheya's lap, an insect bites Radheya, who starts bleeding profusely but does not move, out of duty and for fear of disturbing his teacher. Then Bhargava, the teacher, awakes and wonders at Radheya's capacity as a Brahmin to bear pain. He eventually realizes that Radheya cannot possibly be a Brahmin, for only a *kshatriya* and not a Brahmin can bear pain and the sight of blood. Radheya is consequently cursed by his teacher for having spoken falsely, and his lessons come to an end. The curse of the teacher remains valid and its consequences become apparent in Radheya's fight in the war. The story of Radheya's life spans the epic and is important to it. In it we can see how *vaṃa* differentiation is determined by birth alone.

In some cases duty by one's order may be considered of even greater importance than duty by religion. We are told that, because of moral degeneration, the necessity for the first king arose. He was chosen and crowned by the gods, and he was to follow the science of chastisement (*daṇḍanīti*), which was abridged by Shiva. He was asked to abide by *dharma* and punish any man who 'deviates from the path of duty (*dharma*) and to 'maintain the duties (*dharma*) laid down in the Vedas'.[66] Yet we are also told that 'Kings desirous of success are obliged to adopt both kinds of paths, righteous (dharmic) and unrighteous (adharmic)'.[67] The king is also advised against heeding the counsel of a righteous person, as following the path of righteousness may conflict with the king's first aim of protecting his subjects.

Here we may see that, where *dharma* means righteousness, it need not signify *vaṃa dharma*. The ultimate *dharma* of the *Mahābhārata* which is upheld is one that includes all *dharmas*. It is one which includes good and evil (there is no major victory that is won by either side in the battle and Yudhīshthira, who might appear to win, later gives up his throne, which is an action that is not at all in accordance with his class *dharma*). In this context it would be misleading to say that spiritual superiority was asserted, and it would not be accurate to consider equality or inequality in spiritual terms, as we may in other texts. Inequality between orders is evident in the sphere of everyday life and in the larger context of the epic, but it is not applicable to religious salvation.

The position of woman in the *Mahābhārata* is not significantly different from her position in the *śāstras* which were known at the time. This is not surprising when we consider that three books of the *Mahābhārata* contain as many as 260 out of 2,684 shlokas of the *Manusmṛti*.[68] We may accept that *sati*, though known to the epic, was not necessarily recommended.[69] It has been indicated that the difference between women caused by marriage was comparable to the difference between men caused by caste.[70] In the epic, we are told that 'some fathers love the boy more, some the girl'.[71] Hopkins has also indicated that on almost all occasions when girls are mentioned, it is in connection with their marriage. As in the *śāstras*, women in the epic are excluded from sacrifice, feasts to the Manes, fasting and reading the Veda, although there are parts of a song in honour of Agni, which may be used equally for the purification of both sexes. In the later epic we find that all women are secluded, unlike the earlier epic, but that wives are especially watched over. In the Sabhā scene it would appear that the introduction of Draupadi into the hall of men was more outrageous than her forcible disrobing.[72] Perhaps it was the special honour and respect held for women of a specific status, and later all wives, that encouraged seclusion. Would this confirm the statement that 'it is no woman-worship, however, but if properly analysed, man-worship, that, prompts this honour to woman i.e. to the wife for it is the incarnate husband that makes the wife glorious'.[73] This opinion may disregard the general acceptance in Indian culture that a female, as much as a male, was recommended to share his or her life with a partner, and that the wife's place, unlike that of her husband, was ideally within the household.

We may conclude that differences of function within the orders, and also between gender, were recognized and recommended both in the lay and the religious life to varying extents. However, it would be unwise to overlook the context of the war, where a certain social rigidity was probably necessary to ensure the security and welfare of those concerned.

The Dharma Śāstras

It is likely that both the *Mahābhārata* and the Law Book of Manu were contemporaneous creations. However, in the latter text, unlike the former, we are presented with a codification of *dharma* which can be applied to individuals in a particular situation, and claims legal sanction by justifying its maintenance of the universal order. The events enacted in the epic, on the other hand, take place in a non-human world and are probably more removed from the practical realities of society at the time. In the period of *Smṛti* literature (from approx. 500 BC to AD 500), we have much legal material that refers to discrimination on an order, caste and gender basis for purposes of jurisprudence and punishment (*daṇḍa*) which varied accordingly. The nature of this discrimination may appear harsher today than it was perhaps intended to be, and it is necessary to remember that these texts probably represented the prescriptive more than the descriptive.

The *Śāstras* were based on highly ritualistic *Griya Sūtras*, which upheld a rigid Brahmanic social structure. The *śāstras* were primarily used for teaching students of the twice-born orders and thus must have contributed considerably to moulding attitudes, whether the injunctions laid down were enforceable or not. One may account for the inflexibility of the lawbooks concerning order and gender when considering that these texts were not only based on the *Sūtras*, but were also composed in times of internal turmoil, when a reintegration of non-Aryan-speaking tribes was taking place, and when a Brahmanic revival in the country ensured a certain stability and security in the political, social and religious spheres.

Differences of order or caste by birth indicated both the moral behaviour expected of a person and the suggested punishment. Thus we see how the punishment for murder varies according to class. The fines were: 1,000 cows for killing a *kshatriya*; 100 for killing a *Vaiśya*, and ten cows for killing a *Śūdra* or a woman of any class.[74] Similarly, it was considered more disgraceful and unacceptable for a member of higher order to thieve than for one of a lower order. So, by Manu, the *Śūdra* was required to pay a fine eight times the value of the stolen goods, and the *vaiśya*, the *kṣatriya* and *brāhmaṇa* should pay sixteen, thirty-two and sixty-four times the value of the goods, respectively.[75] In the Vedic period, the Brahmins claimed to be beyond the law, and we know that at times the priestly orders claimed many privileges from the law. According to most orthodox sources, the Brahmins were excluded from capital punishment and torture, although the worst punishment for them was to have the topknot cut off. In practice, this indicated a loss of order, and thus perhaps the right of the law to punish them more severely on subsequent occasions if necessary. The śāstric attitude to orders and castes may be exaggerated in relation to reality if we do not consider the validity of guilds and customary law at the time. Guilds, which had existed at least since about 600 BC, were at their most powerful in the third or fourth century AD. In Manu, we are told that a king is advised to enforce his own laws after a thorough investigation of the 'laws of castes and districts, guild laws and family laws'.[76]

We also have examples of young men who were free to learn a trade, regardless of caste barriers. The earlier *Smṛtis* do not insist on the harmony of customary law and the law of the sacred books, although the later *Smṛtis* appear to prefer this. It is not the place here to determine how far customary law was given precedence over sacred law, but the importance of the validity of customary law, which could be incorporated into written, sacred law, serves to remind us that a certain flexibility in upholding and enforcing sacred law was necessary, and probably desirable.

Woman in all the *Śāstras* was ideally seen as a wife and a mother of sons. Although marriageable age and attitudes to the widow varied in the lawbooks, there is a general agreement on the necessity of the dependence of the wife on her husband for both her material and spiritual welfare. The subordination of woman to man can be seen in the attitude to her position in the *Manuśmṛti*.

> She should do nothing independently
> even in her own house
> In childhood subject to her father,
> in youth to her husband
> and when her husband is dead, to her sons,
> She should never enjoy independence . . .

> Though he be uncouth and prone to pleasure,
> though he has no good points at all,
> the virtuous wife should ever
> worship her lord as a god.

Women were discouraged from taking over the religious life, although they were permitted to do so. They were not allowed to officiate as priests, or to have access to the most sacred texts. The main objective of a wife was to serve her husband, and Manu tells us that 'if a wife obeys her husband, she will for that reason alone be exalted in heaven'. The validity of divorce was not recognized in the early *Śāstras*. The remarriage of widows was not unknown, though ideally a widow was obliged to live with the welfare of the dead husband in mind, and therefore had to impose strict rules on herself, which meant leading a life like that of an ascetic. This attitude to widows was prevalent between about the second and fourth centuries AD. She was considered to be inauspicious to all except her own children. A widower, however, may after his wife's death marry again and again according to the *Manuśmṛti*. Between about the fifth and ninth centuries AD, *sati* became an option for the widow, though Medātithi condemned it. The poet Bāna mentions that the practice of *anumaraṇa* or taking one's life was not confined only to widows, and many stone inscriptions show that it was prevalent in North and South India in about the eleventh century. Most, though not all, authorities deny the rights of women to inherit and, according to the *Arthaśāstra*, the husband had almost unlimited rights over his wife's property. However, when a woman died, it is known that her property would pass not to her husband or her sons but to her daughters. This indicates a fusion with South Indian (Dravidian) matriarchal notions. Although the female's place was confined to being within the household, we have indications that she was considered valuable and precious. Thus we are told that a wife should not on any account be abandoned, for 'to forsake her is not prescribed by the sacred law'.[77] We are also told that one should regard 'one's slaves as one's shadow, one's daughter as the highest object of tenderness';[78] hence, if one is offended by anyone of these, one must bear it without resentment.

Jurists in classical times appear to have been as concerned with the after-life of the accused as they were with the present life. The *śastras* remained as the basis of jurisprudence until and to a limited extent after the coming of the Muslims. It is, however, almost impossible to say which parts of the *śastra* were enforced in practice. To this day, the *Dharmaśāstras* have remained important to scholars. These texts were considered normative by the British, who may have been responsible for making them more rigid than they probably were in reality. The consolidation of the *śastras* by the British through their acknowledgement of the pundits has probably resulted in an exaggerated significance of the texts which regarded inequality as being a necessary ingredient of law. What is vital to remember is that, 'apart from litigation the *śastra* maintained a life of its own, with its appeal to conscience which no royal mandate, no legislation could diminish',[79] and it is because of this that śāstric prescriptions are respected to this very day, centuries after their composition.

Conclusion

In this paper we have considered the concept of equality both in lay and religious lives, and underlined criteria which determine equal or unequal potentialities. We have noted how recognition given to the criteria, or equilibrium that is recommended by a particular tradition or traditions, can have varying implications for attitudes to equality. There has been little discussion on the relevance of these textual traditions to the society of today. Yet, we cannot disregard the value of ancient texts in the modern world, when considering that Vedic hymns are still used for ritual purposes, scenes from the *Mahābhārata* are still enacted on the stage during festive seasons, prescriptions of the *śāstras* appear to be effective guides of the individual conscience and customary law, and *bhakti* is the form of worship most prevalent amongst Hindus today.

Despite certain similarities, it is evident that one clear uniform theory of equality cannot be extracted from the existing Hindu and Buddhist texts that have been examined, though current theories of equality can, in most cases, be derived from these traditions. Thus it is very necessary to acknowledge that these ideas co-exist today within their religious systems, and that similar attitudes to equality prevail within traditions even though they are intrinsically very different from one another. It would be inaccurate to define a general theory of equality also on the grounds of the different social milieux and historical circumstances in which the various beliefs gained popularity. The pluralistic nature of Indian society today needs to be acknowledged and accepted, when considering it in the light of modern concepts of equality and justice.

We need to perceive that there is a problem not just in religion, but also in the domain of economics, law and politics, of the dichotomy between the ideal and the prescribed as opposed to the actual and the described. There is a necessity to understand that if equality exists only as a phenomenon, outside the awareness of the majority of people, it cannot be realized by them. Thus there is a need for the practical aim of creating a human awareness of it from within the traditions concerned and relating the concept to the modern world.

In the Christian and later Western tradition we have a man-centred world outlook, that has been conducive to thinking in human rights terms. In most Indian religious traditions, although human beings are considered a superior species, they are not fundamentally different from lower forms of life; the human may be reborn as an animal, and vice versa. This attitude may account for the categorization of oppressed castes or groups of humans with animal forms of life. In the history of natural law and of human rights, we come across a different problem concerning equality in the man-centred world. This is because of a tension caused between the concept of man or the human represented as a collective group and as an individual entity.

Professor I.C. Sharma, in his essay on 'Human Rights and Comprehensive Humanism',[80] has explained why man cannot be categorized as a religious animal alone, or a political animal or an economic animal alone. He has shown how this could lead to a 'lopsided aspect of human nature'. We may conclude by saying that humans in both the collective and the individual sense are actually entangled in a complex universalist web which incorporates all these aspects and perhaps more which we still have to discover in the course of time.

4 The Concept of Equality in the Theravada Buddhist Tradition

Padmasiri de Silva

Prelude

The importance of the concept of 'equality' in the modern world emerges against the background of the resurgence of interest in the doctrine of human rights. An added facet of this interest has been the discussion pertaining to the question whether human rights are in fact universal and whether they are relevant to non–Western societies with different cultural and religious traditions.

While this paper will focus attention on the Theravāda Buddhist tradition, we shall be concerned with the following questions:

1. Concepts of equality are coloured by the kind of emphasis given in different historical contexts and this fact is even more visible when they emerge within the framework of religious and ethical systems. What are the kinds of variable which give specific form and shape to Buddhist reflections on equality? What is the kind of world-view which gives meaning and direction to Buddhist thinking on the subject of equality and related concepts? How is the equality concept in the Buddhist tradition 'grounded'? What is the kind of centrality it has in the light of its world-view?

2. While being aware of these specific variables, do we discern a clear profile about Buddhist thinking on the subject? The sermons of the Buddha (first preserved in an oral tradition and written down later) offer diverse contexts of relevant material. What is the total impact when these contexts are put together?

3. Is there a kind of perennial philosophy in these texts which gives us some light to understand the link between these historical contexts and modern times? If discussions on 'equality' today in the West are subject to a kind of ethnocentric bias and if rethinking on the conceptualization of human rights is necessary, what contributions can a forum on equality in the religious and cultural traditions of Asia make to the ongoing debate?

It may not be possible to discuss all these questions in detail, but if some of these questions can be raised and others examined in more detail we should make some progress. A recent study entitled 'Human Rights: A Western Construct with Limited Applicability' makes the following observation:

> It is becoming increasingly evident that the Western political philosophy upon which the [UN] Charter and Declaration [of Human Rights] are based provides only one particular interpretation of human rights, and that this Western notion may not be successfully applicable to non-Western areas for several reasons ... cultural differences whereby philosophic underpinnings defining human nature and the relationship of individuals to others and to society are markedly at variance with Western individualism.[1]

This attempt to study religious traditions of Asia should help us to make some contribution to the problem of cultural and ideological ethnocentrism in the province of the study of human rights.

In this context it would be of great interest to note that Buddhism has a world-view coloured by an ethical and spiritual message; its reflections are not focused on the limited life span of an individual or society but the cycle of existence where concepts of rebirth and *kamma* figure prominently; above the ever-changing socio-political order, there is a cosmic order; the content of human rights, like the right to life and security, emerges through concepts of obligation and duties in the Buddhist context; Buddhism emphasizes the role of the individual for the purpose of attaining liberation but the idea of 'reciprocity' and reciprocal human relations (as found in the paradigmatic *Sigālovāda Sutta*) introduces the framework of mutual obligations; questions of human needs and freedom are examined in the light of a central ideal — the blend of material and spiritual progress. While Buddhism has universal concerns relating to human rights which converge on the Western pursuit, these variables add a special flavour to Buddhist thinking on human rights in general and equality in particular.

The fact that Buddhist reflections on equality, especially those pertaining to caste and women, are grounded in ethico-religious contexts has, however, been misunderstood by some, giving the idea that they have little socio-political relevance. It is true that the vibrant centre of the Buddha's teaching was an ethical and religious message, but paradoxically this makes its relevance for social transformation even greater. The Buddhist concept of equality has a strong moral flavour. Finally, as compassion and benevolence played a great role in the Buddhist attitude to man's problems, the approach to human rights is basically 'humanistic' rather than 'legalistic'. Thus, as you make an entry into the Buddhist world-view, you discover the ingredients which colour its perspectives on human rights, and in certain senses there is an ethos, a way of looking at things, different from the reigning Western stance.

Now that we have outlined the directions of our thinking, we shall proceed with the detailed examination, which will fall into two parts: a section dealing with Buddhist world-view orientations and reflections on equality, and another dealing with the dimensions of equality like the analysis of the place of caste and women in Buddhist thought. In the concluding section we shall briefly sum up the direction of our discussion and point towards a more constructive pathway.

Buddhist world-view orientation and the concept of equality

Religion can be so deeply integrated into social life, as in ancient India, that it is difficult to isolate it as a distinct phenomenon. In the context of the Buddhist tradition, it is not limited to a ritual, ethical or social aspect but involves a world-view orientation which pervades diverse aspects of life. Before the appearance of Islam, the pre-Buddhistic Hindu tradition and Buddhism presented relatively different world-views, though as non-Western perspectives there were points of convergence between them. When we use the term 'non-Western', it is necessary to understand some of the finer distinctions within its own fold and especially within the Indian tradition itself. Also, due to the strong power of absorption and tolerance found within Hinduism as such, the distinctive Buddhist contribution has been lost to the Western student of human rights immersed in generalizations.

Sramanism and Brahmanism represent the two great religious philosophies of India in ancient times. The sources of early Brahmanism include the *Samhitās*, *Brāhmaṇas*, the *Āraṇyakas* and the oldest *Upaniṣads*. The non-Vedic origin of the *Upaniṣads* has been a point of great controversy.[2] It has been suggested that yoga, Sāṃkhya, early Jainism and some of the extra-ordinary ideas of the *Upaniṣads* had a common sramanic origin.[3] The great doctrines concerning *yoga*, *dhyāna*, *karma*, *ahimsa*, *mokṣa* and *saṃsāra* seem to have been the legacy of *munis* or *sramanas*, 'ascetic sages'. Sakyamuni the great *sramaṇa* disregarded the priestly ritualism, the sacrifices and the system of fixed castes (*yannas*). Over the years in India, the apparent distinctiveness of these traditions became partly confused due to the strong integrative power of Hinduism, and especially with the emergence of the Vedānta of Śankara certain blends between Sramanism and Brahmanism emerged. The early Buddhist tradition, however, took root in Sri Lanka, Thailand, Burma, and also in Laos, Vietnam and Cambodia, and the later traditions of Buddhism took root in Japan, China, Korea, Tibet and Mongolia.[4]

In fact, it is an easier task to discern the impact of Buddhism on modern socio-political thought of these countries than in India due to the integrating power of Hinduism and also its eclectic nature. Some of the great figures in recent Indian history like Gandhi, Jawaharlal Nehru, Vinobha Bhave, Rabindranath Tagore and Krishnamurthi exhibit the tremendous impact of the personality, philosophy and lifestyle of the Buddha on their thinking. In the words of a recent scholar, referring to the feelings of Indian leaders regarding the decline of Buddhism in India:

> They have resented that Buddhism declined in India; they have reaffirmed the Buddhist tradition of religious tolerance; they have criticised the existence of those very customs and institutions in their own tradition which were first criticised by the Buddha and the Buddhists. Caste system, priestly laws, feudal customs, untouchability, social disabilities of women, and the like, all these elements of traditional Brahmanical heritage have been attacked and reformed, at least in theory.[5]

Thus it is said that the constitution of the Indian Republic has been inspired by the Buddha and the 'wheel of righteousness' on the national flag of India is a symbol of the Buddha's message of wisdom and compassion. Thus one who attempts to assess the place of Buddhism in the Indian ideological, cultural and religious heritage will come across cross-cutting points of convergence and divergence. The world-views of Islam and Christianity have been placed as alternative conceptions by those who regard both Hinduism and Buddhism within the 'Old Asian' world perspective. Ninian Smart, who makes an analysis and an 'Inventory of Worldviews' refers to the following major orientations: the Marxist Bloc, the Islamic Crescent, Old Asia, the Latin World, black Africa and the Pacific.[6] To take one important doctrinal strand, the religions of Judaism, Christianity and Islam, which all hark back to Abraham and the prophets, do not accept reincarnation. Rebirth or reincarnation form a central component of the Hindu-Buddhist doctrinal axis.

This is, of course, not the place to do an exhaustive analysis of the comparative study of these different world-views, but it must be emphasized that attention must be paid as to how these perspectives influence all aspects of life, including socio-political reflections.

As an example of the relationship of world-views and socio-political thought, let us take something connected to the issues of caste, the concepts of rebirth and *Kamma*. Both Buddhism and Hinduism accept the existence of a moral order. In spite of the differences between the two systems, the concept of *dharma* provides a common non-Western perspective. As Smart observes: 'Although Hinduism often involves belief in one divine being, it shares with Buddhism a sense that the law or *dharma* is not something which is commanded by God, but rather it is a part of the world.'[7] While Hinduism makes the caste system itself controlled by this order, Buddhism does not see any moral or rational basis for caste. The Buddha has, of course, said that among the conditions that determine rebirth in lower castes, the result of previously done actions of an evil nature (*kamma*) is admitted as one of the possible explanations.[8] But the Buddha did not embrace fatalism by saying that mere birth (*jāti*) decided for good a man's position and role in life. Man's conduct in this life is even more important than the result of his past actions.

In actual practice it is possible that people project a sense of fatalism into the *kamma* notion but this is due to wrong understanding. The term *kamma* generally means that one's moral acts will bear fruit in this life as well as the other life. But there are two strands in the *kamma* concept, both of which are important, and they may be referred to as the 'judicial model' and the 'craftsmanship model'. In the Middle Length Sayings it is said that if an individual resorts to killing living creatures, steals, resorts to sexual misconduct, and so on, he will be born in a sorrowful state of existence; the one who practices kindness to animals, one who is merciful, compassionate, restrains himself and guards his senses, is born in a happy state or heavenly world.[9]

But apart from the just dispensation of rewards and punishment, there is also a craftsmanship model of *kamma* which emphasizes the self-creating and self-perfecting (or self-degrading) nature of actions and continued disposition for good or bad. The concept of the deed as an expression of one's character is the one that throws light on the craftsmanship model of *kamma*. On the one hand, action reflects the agent's character, and on the other hand, repeated action increases the disposition to act in the same manner. The greatest blessing of a good action is the tendency to repeat similar deeds.

It is in this light that Buddhism rejects both fatalism and the stagnant structures of caste based on divine sanctions. Men should put aside distinctions related to birth or profession and place supreme emphasis on moral conduct: 'A man is noble or ignoble through conduct, but not through birth.'[10] In emphasizing the importance of moral conduct, rejecting fatalism and theories of determinism and focusing on man's free will, in appealing to man's power of reason (see *Kālāma Sutta*),[11] and basically pointing towards the potentiality for good and bad within everyone, the Buddha upheld a notion of equality within the ethical and spiritual fold.

The Buddhist concept of the cosmic order and its conception of human potentiality, its ethics and its spiritual quest form the basic facets of its world-view orientation. This conception is again stabilized by its methodological perspectives, which emphasize rational examination of any views based on superstition and habit, confrontation with empirical situations and an experiential and humanistic approach to problems. This perspective has generated interesting views about man's social concerns and some of these threads will be put together in the following section.

The equality concept in Buddhism

The core of the Buddha's teaching was an ethical and spiritual message, as his main concern was the sense of unsatisfactoriness (*dukkha*), which lies at the base of the perilous human condition of unrest, anguish and ignorance. Reflections on society and polity emerged as a supplement to this concern. But this does not in any way mean that the Buddha was not concerned about the transformation of society, it only means that his approach to social concerns had a logic of its own, as also the analysis of concepts like freedom, equality and justice.

The Buddha did not say that social change was unnecessary, but that this could not be achieved merely by restructuring social organizations, as along with this a basic transformation of the individual was necessary. Basically, the Buddha saw the strongest links between ethics and society and ethics and politics, and this whole dimension is summed up in the Buddhist conception of justice, which may be rendered by the term *righteousness,* a notion which colours Buddhist thinking on equality. There was also a sense of pragmatism and practicality in the Buddha, who accepted the institution of kingship as it existed in that society but tried to enhance this seat of power and authority by guiding it on the principles of sound, fair and righteous rule. Above the social and political order was the Buddhist concept of *dharma*, the cosmic order in the universe, and the king had not merely to respect this order but also, as the 'wheel-turning monarch', to see that this order was reflected in his regime. This is the special sense in which the Buddhist concept of justice (righteousness) reverberates within the socio-political scheme and relates in an interesting manner to the Buddhist concept of equality.

As the notion of equality in relation to caste and the position of women has often been discussed in the sermons in religious contexts like the entry into the order and the potential for liberation, there has been a tendency to neglect its socio-political contexts. In the contexts where the Buddha advises kings and ministers we get some interesting interventions.

A king's economic policy should be guided by a sense of 'equity' and this, as Wijesekera points out, can be inferred from 'the parallel qualifications of the righteous king's rule by *dhammena* and *samena* with equally significant emphasis'.[12] 'The latter word, going back to a base "sama", meaning equality, is in its juristic aspect used to indicate impartiality and fair play'. It is said that when levying taxes the king should, apart from imposing taxes to run the state, consider the plight of those who are subject to the taxes. There are even instances where a righteous king, in order to redress the poverty of some, had fresh taxes laid on the wealthy and the wealth distributed among the needy. *Dāna*, or giving to those who need, is a function of the righteous king. The Buddha discouraged greed and acquisition, encouraged moderate savings for the future, condemned both hoarding and waste and recommended charity and liberality. The impelling motive of benevolence was stronger than any concept of distributive justice as such. In the political contexts we know that the Buddha requested the representatives of the Vajjian republic to respect their constitution and hold regular meetings in amity and concord. In general the *cakkavatti* or the universal monarch should govern justly and impartially (*dhammena samena*). It has been mentioned that the three components of righteousness are (i) impartiality, (ii) just requital and (iii) truthfulness. The Buddhist concept of equality works within this framework.[13]

The main strands in the Buddhist equality concept are:

(i)   Rejection of artificial and arbitrary distinctions among human beings, rejection of caste distinctions based on birth and emphasis on character.

(ii) Common human potentialities:

    (a) spirituality and moral transformation;
    (b) rationality;
    (c) ability to feel for others' suffering;
    (d) free will;
    (e) presence of secular skills.

(iii) All beings (including animals) are subject to common human predicament, which may be broadly called *dukkha* — unsatisfactoriness. Birth, sickness and death are the great levellers.

(iv) The great cosmic order which rules all beings, concepts of rebirth and *kamma*.

    (a) The Buddhist concept of rewards and punishment or just requital at the cosmic level (the judicial model).
    (b) The strength of dispositional activity (the craftsmanship notion).
    (c) Implementation of the just and righteous rule by the 'wheel-turning monarch'.

(v) The concept of human dignity and equal respect for all (*samānattatā*); Buddha's attitude to Ambapali (a moral outcast), Angulimala (a criminal), Rukkas (a social outcast), and the diversity of personality types and the diversity of vocations from which his adherents came.

(vi) Basic needs and the conditions for self-development.

(vii) An expression of boundless compassion and benevolence (equality notions fed by a humanistic rather than a legalistic conscience).

Some of these strands of the equality concept have been put together to get a clearer and more comprehensive vision of the discussion on equality in the Buddhist context. There is some overlapping, as in the case of items (i) and (v); there were also other facets which emerged later in the history of this concept. The Asokan empire, for instance, brought to the surface the question of equality in a multi-religious context. There are certain significant variables which made the Buddhist discussion of equality a little different from its Western counterpart. This last point is important and should be briefly discussed before we clarify other dimensions of the equality concept in the next section. The major variable in the equality discussion in Buddhism is the notion of reciprocity, where certain desirable goals are to be attained through the notion of duties and obligations rather than rights; thus, in the *Sigālovāda Sutta*, what is discussed is the way in which man as husband, father and master, and woman as wife, mother and mistress of the house perform diverse functions which are reciprocated. Instead of raising questions of equality in relation to man and woman, we find how they supplement and complement each other. In fact, over the years, other communal and organic relationships going beyond the family have emerged, especially in countries like Sri Lanka, where the temple-centred village communities have emerged. This is an extremely important variable highlighted in recent non-Western presentations of equality.

The *Sigālovāda Sutta* discusses the distribution of duties in six types of relationship: parents and children, pupil and teacher, husband and wife, householder and friend, employer and employee, and householder to a *samana*. From these let us take the husband and wife relationship. A wife should be ministered to by her husband in five ways — by being courteous to her, by not despising her, by being faithful to her, by handing over authority to her and by providing her with necessary adornments; the wife should minister to her husband in five ways — by ordering the household well, by hospitality to their relatives, by fidelity, by taking care of his wealth and by her industry. In the same manner they have functions as mother and father, as neighbour and friend, employer, and so on.[14]

This concept is important when we examine the place of women in Buddhism, and in this context the equality concept loses its sting. The question emerges in relation to the admission of women to the order and the assessment of their potentiality for spiritual transformation. The concept of reciprocity is a certain socio-cultural type well exhibited in traditional Chinese moral life and Confucian discourse about 'rules of proper conduct'. To cite the moral virtues listed in the *Li Chi*:

> Kindness on the part of the father, and the filial duty on that of the son; gentleness on the part of the elder brother, and obedience on the younger; righteousness on the part of the husband, and submission on that of the wife; kindness on the part of elders, and deference on that of juniors; with benevolence (*jen*) on the part of the ruler, and loyalty on that of the minister. These ten are the things which men consider to be right.[15]

With reference to the nature of these rules of proper conduct, it has been said that the notion of 'rights' 'does not find a comfortable home in Confucian ethics'.[16] This point is important as this feature has not been well emphasized and placed in a non-Western perspective in some of the very recent discussions of human rights in the Buddhist tradition. It is necessary that we look at the human rights tradition in the West from the bases of our religious, ethical and cultural perspectives. Even the Buddhist five precepts which embody the content of some of the human rights like the right to life and property are not presented in the form of rights, commandments, injunctions, and so on. They are presented in the form of a promise (or even duty) such that they ensure the basic conditions of harmonious social life and the development of individual character. In the same manner the duties of the universal monarch to his subjects and the obligations of the subjects are discussed in the *suttas*.[17]

Normative and factual aspects of the equality concept

A question which has often been raised in the modern analysis of the equality concept is whether it is grounded in facts or values. While it often takes the form of a principle of procedure, a maxim to guide action and an ideal to be approximated, there is often an appeal to facts, and this is especially so in the appeal to a common human nature. The idea is that behind all differences of talent, merits and social advantage, there is some characteristically human nature in terms of which all men can be considered equal.

The appeal to common humanity is a central facet in the Buddhist analysis of the equality concept, and though the assertion that men are alike in possessing certain truly human traits sounds like a tautology, it is of great importance to equality perspectives fed by strong humanistic overtones, as in Buddhism. It really combines a factual claim regarding traits of human nature and the edifying call of a normative nature to develop these potentialities. Bernard Williams in his essay on 'The Idea of Equality' refers to the 'capacity to feel pain' and the 'capacity to feel affection for others' as important ingredients in the understanding of man's common humanity. 'The assertion that men are alike in the possession of these characteristics is, while indisputable and (it may be) even necessarily true, not trivial. For it is certain that there are political and social arrangements that systematically neglect these characteristics in the case of some groups of men.'[18] Thus, if political and social arrangements neglect moral claims which arise from these characteristics, they are not satisfactory. In a very deep sense, the need to be 'respected as a human person' and the ability to respond to others as human persons provides the most basic moral and psychological foundations for Buddhist reflections on equality.

Though there may be individual differences, there is a basic similarity in the material, psychological and spiritual needs of man; it is both a fact to be respected and a norm to be recommended. If we take the Buddha's rejection of caste distinctions, on the one hand it is recommended as a norm that men should put aside distinctions related to birth and place greater emphasis on conduct; it has also a factual component that, in the just dispensation of rewards and punishments in the cosmic moral order, conduct rather than birth is respected. It is of course a fact of a special kind, different from the general routine empirical facts. Like the ability to feel for the suffering of others, man's rationality, the presence of free will, the potentiality for spiritual and moral transformation all have a factual core which gets blended with normative considerations. They are perhaps 'idealized capacities' of man. Women were considered as equal in having these potentialities, and in the case of compassion, a mother's feelings towards a child is taken as the paradigmatic expression of human compassion.

Egalitarianism, of course, does not always assert equality but rather denies the justice of some inequality in treatment based on irrelevant traits. In this context, the dimensions of equality in relation to race, caste, sex, and so on, are important. Buddhist reflections on caste distinctions and the place of women will be taken for discussion in the next section.

Summing up

Before we begin our analysis of the dimensions of equality in the Buddhist tradition, it may be useful to sum up our findings regarding the equality concept as such. As far as the Buddhist concept of equality is concerned, it has a strong link with the notion of righteousness (*dhamma*), which may be rendered for the Western student as *justice*, but yet in a narrow sense it is a Buddhist concept of justice or, in a more broader sense, a notion of justice embedded in the Hindu-Buddhist world-view.

The interlocking relations between justice and equality have been a subject of great interest in recent studies of equality in the West. In early Greek thought, for instance, the word *dike* (which came to mean a person's due share) implicitly contained the concept of equality, thus showing an interesting link between justice and equality. In the Buddhist context we have shown the strong link between righteousness and equality in relation to the way a king should govern;

dhammena and *samena* are used to describe the qualifications of an ideal king.

Within the Buddhist world-view the notion of righteousness manifests itself at a number of levels. First, the moral and cosmic order, which evaluates people in terms of their normal moral conduct rather than their birth, wealth or position, and administers the just dispensation of rewards and punishments, is a great 'leveller'. Second, the wheel-turning monarch is expected to reflect the principles of righteousness in his regime and thus practice the ideals of impartiality and fairness and in general encourage the people to practice these ideas themselves along with other virtues like veracity and benevolence. Third, the individual is expected to follow the principle of righteousness in his daily life and help in the stabilization of a righteous regime and also develop human relationships and group relations on the same principle. In short, the Buddhist concept of justice as 'righteousness' has a strong moral basis instead of mere legal or political overtones. Buddhist equality notions are nurtured within this world-view.

Thus, in the first instance, the strong link between righteousness and equality has to be noticed. Secondly, the Buddhist perspective on equality is basically orientated towards the human person as a free and rational moral agent. Thirdly, treating persons as equals in this respect indicates that we value common human potentialities. Fourthly, the moral imperative to treat others in the same way as one would wish oneself to be treated assumes that we are in certain ways equal. Finally, this perspective is rooted in our deep emotional capacity for benevolence and compassion.

Some dimensions of equality in Buddhism

The preceding examination of the concept of equality was not a historical study regarding the evolution of the equality concept in the Indian tradition; neither was it a descriptive and sociological study. Our primary task was analytical, to lay bare the main strands in the Buddhist equality concept and place it against the specific variables and the world-view orientation which colour reflections on equality in the Buddhist tradition, and, along with this, to explore the possibility of finding a non-Western perspective on human rights. While historical and sociological studies can enrich our deliberations, the kind of ground clearing we attempted by this analysis should have its own legitimate place in a multi-disciplinary forum.

In line with this, we shall examine some of the types of context and the kinds of arguments the Buddha used in criticizing the institution of caste, and this will be done using the available textual material in the sermons of the Buddha.

The Buddha attempted to show in significant contexts that there was no absolute sanction about caste gradations and that there was no need to assume that they have any sacred or divine sanction. For instance, the Buddha once told King Kosala that, in times of a crisis, as in the case of a war, he would be forced to enlist in his army not only men of the warrior caste but also others, provided they were well trained, in spite of the fact that they may be drawn from the *kṣatriya*, *vaiśya* or *śūdra* family. Here the Buddha was pointing towards the relative nature of these distinctions in a very clear empirical situation.[19]

A similar argument used to show the relative nature of these distinctions is found in the *Madhura Sutta*, where it is said that if a person is wealthy, irrespective of his caste, he will find that members of other castes will wait upon him and serve him.[20] It is interesting to find the Buddha using this kind of argument. He is not saying that wealth *should be* the norm which divides man, but merely that in actual situations, birth and colour (*vanna*) recede to the background in the face of wealth.

In fact this argument regarding wealth as a factor which influences social relations is strengthened by three other arguments: a wicked man (whatever his *vanna*), in accordance with the law of *kamma*, will be born in a bad place and a good man in a state of bliss; a criminal, whatever his *vanna*, will be equally subject to punishment for his crime; also, whatever a man's *vanna*, if he joins the order, he will receive equal respect and honour from people. The second argument is used in terms of the cosmic moral order to which we have referred to earlier; the third is interesting as it refers to the legal context, and the final one to the religious context. It is necessary to keep in mind these diverse arguments as some scholars have overemphasized the religious context regarding admission to the order. This is an important context, but the Buddha had a more comprehensive and complex case against caste.

In the same way that the Buddha was critical of the alleged absoluteness of caste distinctions, he was critical of the fatalism which was often associated with it. It is true that the Buddha admitted that, among the factors which influence a man's birth in a lower caste, previously done bad *kamma* may be one. The Buddha, however, did not embrace fatalism by saying that mere birth decided for good a man's place and position in life. The Buddha avoids both theories of determinism with a fatalistic flavour and theories of indeterminism which see the emergence of events as accidents. The fatalistic view considers the experiences of a man as the result of previous actions and *totally* determined by them (*pubbekatahetu*), or if not, determined by some divine plan (*issaranimmanahetu*). According to strict determinism, the present and the future are dependent on the past and therefore unalterable, or every event is predetermined in the light of a divine plan. Free will in the Buddhist context means the ability of a person to control the dynamic forces of the past and present and make the future different from what it would otherwise have been.

Apart from emphasizing the free will concept in relation to the individual, the Buddha also encourages his followers to look at history, the sense of dynamism involved in the evolution of society. This evolutionary concept of society, though presented in the form of a myth in the *Aggañña Sutta*[21] and also developed in the *Cakkavattisīhanāda Sutta*[22] in the form of a legend, presents a model of social change in comparison with the more static picture of the universe which prevailed at the time. Not only does the Buddha say that changes can be seen in a dynamic evolutionary setting but also that, in a larger time-scale in a cyclic setting, Buddhism accepts the fact of change and flux as a part of the nature of things. It is also said that laws are not haphazard. There are laws which pertain to the natural world as well as the psychological and social, and these may be described as 'non–deterministic social correlations'. Ideas, ideologies as well as economic factors influence the paths of social change. In this process of change, the moral factor plays a crucial role, and good and bad are qualities not determined in terms of caste distinctions. 'Now seeing, Vāseṭṭha, that both bad and good qualities, blamed and praised respectively by the wise, are thus distributed among each of the four classes, the wise do not admit those claims which the brahmins put forward.'[23] Scholars feel that, though built up in the form of a fanciful myth, the *Aggañña Sutta* has some interesting insights into social evolution and is 'much nearer the truth' than the Brahmin legend it was intended to replace.

Here again, we see that though matters like equality in relation to the admission to order and the potential for religious development made the stand on caste important in the religious context, the Buddha's vindication of the anti-caste perspective emerged from a wider world-view orientation.

We have seen that the Buddha emphasized the relativity of the caste distinctions as compared with the belief in divine sanction and sacredness; it was also pointed out that the element of fatalism which came into being with caste beliefs was put aside in favour of human free will, and a dynamic and evolutionary concept of social change was suggested instead of a rigid and static picture of the world. Another interesting aspect of Buddha's discussions on caste is that in certain contexts the Buddha directly appealed to man's rationality. The Buddha says in the *Vāseṭṭha Sutta* that, though there are species among plants and animals, among human beings there are no such distinctions. Even if there are minor differences regarding the colour of the hair, skin or shape of the head there are no characteristics indicating differences of species (*lingaṃ jātimayaṃ*) among human beings. Though constructed in the form of an analogical reasoning there is a direct appeal to man's confrontation with visible facts and their implications.

This argument has received a good deal of discussion in relation to the very pointed resemblance we find between race prejudice and caste prejudice:

> The phenomenon of caste in India, if only due to its uniqueness, is probably to be traced to a multiplicity of factors, some of which are peculiar to the Indian context, but much of caste prejudice probably had its origin in the racial prejudices of the race-conscious fair-skinned Aryans trying to suppress and administer the dark-skinned aborigines. In any case, the analogy between race prejudice and discrimination and the prejudice and discrimination within the hierarchy of castes is so close that the case against the former is applicable to the latter — and vice versa.[24]

Apart from the intrinsic irrationality of racial and caste-orientated thinking, it had grave practical consequences like the possible denial of political and economic equality, equality before the law and also religious freedom. The study of these practical contexts and the socio-economic role of the caste system over the years in India (or even in Sri Lanka) goes beyond the analytically-orientated theoretical study envisaged in this chapter.

Another facet of the critique of caste in Buddhism is to be found in the references to the psychological foundations of prejudice and the roots of caste and racial conceit. While *suttas* like the *Assalayana Sutta* of the *Majjhima Nikāha* break through the deluded collective arrogance of caste groups, and while the sermon uses both commonsensical reflections and rational arguments for this purpose, the psychological facets of this issue are important. Though the Buddhist contribution to the psychological roots of the issue is very significant, it has been a badly neglected subject with the textual-orientated studies of caste in Buddhism. Feelings of 'identity' (as compared with uncritical and compulsive mechanisms of 'identification') have a temporary role from a Buddhist perspective; they can give a sense of direction and coherence, so long as we are aware of the limited goals of seeking a national identity in socio-political contexts, but we should not let this expand into an inflated and uncritical conceit. Like individuals, nations can develop a healthy sense of patriotism or love for the country, but they can also develop damaging narcissistic self-images of a fanatical type and this factor is all the more important in pluralistic contexts where there are different religious, ethnic, linguistic and caste identities.[25] While majority groups can develop uncritical identities, minority groups can be nourished by feelings of inferiority conceits or even equality conceits.

According to the Buddha, self-conceit takes three forms: I am superior to others (*seyyo 'ham asmi-māna*), I am equal to the others (*sadiso 'ham asmi-māna*), I am inferior to others (*hino 'ham asmi-māna*). *Māna* can range from a crude feeling of pride to a subtle feeling of distinctiveness. Pride, vanity and conceit can emerge in interpersonal as well as inter-group situations. It can emerge in relation to one's physical appearance, birth, intelligence, wealth, as well as caste or race (*jātimada*).

Women, family and the religious quest

Buddhist discussions about the role of women in relation to the notion of equality can often be misplaced, as the contexts in which we raise the question are somewhat different from those of equality notions in relation to caste or race. In the case of the caste concept, the Buddha was critical about it without any equivocation or ambiguity and exposed the pre-Buddhistic rationale for it was untenable. Regarding the position of women in Buddhism, there are two types of context which have to be distinguished. In the case of women, while being critical of any primitive attitudes towards them as the performance of suttee (self-immolation at the husband's funeral pyre), the Buddha was attempting to find out their fitting place amidst the diversity of human relationships, their lifestyles and the contrasting life perspectives of the householder and the recluse. In spite of the great deal of literature available on the subject, an inability to see some of these simple points against their authentic historical background has given an unnecessary twist to the question. In the Confucian ethos (which has great relevance for Buddhist notions of the family), the idea of 'propriety', elegance, sensitivity in human relationships, especially the dimensions of the 'feminine' as well as 'masculine', take a central place. If we take the *Sigālovāda Sutta* as paradigmatic of the Buddhist concept of reciprocity in human relations, the notion of being 'supplementary' or 'complementary' acquires greater centrality than the concept of equality. The concept of equality did emerge in some form, when the question of the admission of women to the order was raised. As far as the potential and the need for liberation from suffering was concerned there was no dispute. The Buddha preached to both men and women and recognized the spiritual potential of women. The second point on which there has been discussion within the Buddhist tradition, especially within the *Mahāyāna* tradition, is the possibility of women attaining Buddhahood, apart from the realization of sainthood or perfection (*arahat*). A third point that has received some discussion is the relative superiority of the formal place of the monk in contrast to that of the nun.

There is a significant difference of perspective in the goals of the householder who aims at righteous and harmonious living (*dhammacariyā, samacariyā*) and the recluse seeking a more immediate form of liberation and inner peace. The householder attempts to be a well-adjusted and balanced person, who, while he seeks pleasure, exercises a degree of restraint, limits his wants and condemns excessive and illegitimate pleasures. While the life of the recluse (*brahmacariyā*) emphasizes the ideal of celibacy, the life of the householder (*gahapati*) emphasizes the idea of chastity. Chastity is an important virtue, and the sanctity of family life and the ideals of conjugal love are upheld in Buddhism. Though polygamy was a prevailing pattern at the time, monogamy fits with the Buddhist ideal. The woman's place within this family contributing to the spiritual aspects is well recognized in the sermons of the Buddha and the literary works which emerged around the doctrine. She brings stability, care, patience and compassion into the home, but is yet capable of dynamism, activity and even physical exertion. With the passage of time Buddhist women have accepted social and political roles but there need not be any special point of tension in this expanding role.

The inability to grasp the distinction between the lifestyle of the householder and the recluse has resulted in misunderstanding the place of women in Buddhism, and especially the place of women in relation to man's sexual life, the blessings of a happy married life and the nature of conjugal love and domestic felicity. To cite one example, the *Encyclopaedia of Religion and Ethics* article discussing women and emancipation in Buddhism comments thus: 'Nor did Buddhism, in spite of its universalism, place a woman on a higher level with man, its highest morality demands entire abstinence from sexual life.'[26] The author of this article fails to realize that, even when women enter the higher life, celibacy is a strict ideal they have to follow. I have discussed Buddhist perspectives on sexuality in detail elsewhere,[27] and do not wish to pursue the subject in detail here.

There are many contexts where the Buddha emphasizes the power of women to attract and excite man, their craft and cunning and their seductive strains which can even match the sensualist in Søren Kierkegaard's *Banquet*.[28] In fact, a Buddhist text comments, 'Inscrutable as the way of a fish in water is the nature of women, those thieves of many devices, with whom truth is hard to find'.[29]

But in spite of all these, the virtues in which they excel and the spiritual heights they attain, as well as the magic power they have in converting a house into a home, are central to a Buddhist perspective on women. It is because the Buddha saw the terrible sense of dissonance and tedium in the life of the pure sensualist (*kāmasukhallikānuyoga*) that he recommended the more balanced family life to both men and women who wish to commit themselves to the life of a householder.

Regarding the granting of religious rights to women the Buddha's contribution was historic. But his initial hesitation when Mahaprajapati Gotami made the request, and made the request three times until with the backing of Ānanda a final request was made which the Buddha granted, . . . is a context which has been the centre of much discussion. When Ānanda asked the Buddha whether women were not capable of a contemplative life and treading the path of arahatship, the Buddha replied that they were certainly capable of gaining arahatship. A plausible answer to this situation has been given:

> This event described in the Pāli Canon as well as Chinese Agamas reveals that Gautama hesitated to permit admission of women in the Order, not because women could not attain enlightenment, but because he had to deliberate on problems which might arise between the Order of monks and that of nuns, and between the Buddhist Order and the lay society.[30]

The Buddha was both a great sage and a great administrator and he acted with great caution.

The hesitation or deliberation was quite natural on his part as the leader of a great number of disciples. We should not interpret this event as showing discrimination against women by Gautama because he never as much as hinted that a woman had not the same chance as a man to become an arahat, or that she was in any way unfit by her nature to attain nirvana.[31]

Regarding the claim that a woman cannot attain Buddhahood as woman in any particular life, this is recorded in the *sutta* literature, and only the Mahāyānists have tried to give a modified interpretation of this claim. In the *Bahudhātukasutta* of the *Majjhima-nikāya* five types of impossibility are cited for a woman: to become a Buddha, Universal Monarch, Mara, Indra or Brahma, while they are within the powers of a man.[32] A similar reference is found in the *Anguttara-nikāya*.[33] Some Mahāyānist scholars consider this as a later addition, which came up probably in the first century BC. We do not hope to pursue this question but merely place these comments on record. Some of the Mahāyānists however infer that according to their interpretations a female can be an aspirant to Buddhahood. What the Theravāda sources indicate is that, in the life in which a person attains Buddhahood, that person has to be a man.

Regarding the moral and spiritual excellence of women, there is a well-documented tradition of references. A considerable section of the poetic utterances of women who attained various grades of spiritual state are found in the *Therīgāthā*. Records of the attainment of árahatship as well as insights into nirvana are found here. Another source for reference is the *Bhikkuni saṁyutta* of the *Saṁyutta-nikāya* and a third is the stories of the Apadāna. Some of the nuns, Shukla, Kundala-Keshi, Bhadra-Kapilani and Dharmadatta, were well-known speakers who gave sermons to large groups. There are many celebrated sections of the *sutta* dealing with the wisdom and moral excellences as well as the predicament of women seeking solace from the Buddha — Queen Mallika, Khema of great wisdom, Kisagotami, Patacara, Ambapali, and so on.[34]

In general, if we take the historical context into account, the profile of woman in the *suttas* is an inspiring as well as a balanced image compared with the image of women in the wild excesses of the Western feminist movement today.

The political and economic contexts of the equality concept

Questions pertaining to equality in the political contexts of today are very different from the simpler issues of the time of the Buddha.

Kingship was the established institution of the time, and it was the king who directed the political, economic and administrative structure of the country. Instead of attempting to reject the institution, the Buddha tried to humanize and elevate its moral stature. The notion that the king should govern with the approval and the consent of the people was the axiom to be followed and a significant phrase used to describe the king was *mahāsammata*: the king is so entitled as he has been selected by the people. He is also expected to govern according to the principles of the *dhamma* and to ensure that the moral and cosmic order of the universe was reflected in his regime, and thus the universal monarch was called the 'wheel-turning monarch'. The king has to maintain stability, peace and ensure the happiness and prosperity of the people. The ideal king in Buddhism is referred to as *dhammika dhammaraja* (righteous lord of righteousness). He rules the people with justice and equity.

There were ten royal virtues which guided the king: generosity; moral conduct; self-sacrifice; honesty and integrity; gentleness and politeness; austerity and simplicity; freedom from hatred and ill will; practice of non-violence; patience; and non-opposition to public welfare.

The people's voice should be effective when the king does not follow these principles, and heredity is not the sole criterion of the genuine successor to kingship. In the simple political framework during the time of the Buddha, concepts of political equality did not have the kind of strong thrust they have today.

Compared with the more simple perspective on politics, Buddhist thoughts on the economic activities of man have a more perennial appeal. We are living in a world which has escalated a crisis of a kind and a world which is evolving its own methodology to intervene in the situation of dilemma it has created.

The Buddha, of course, believes that it is easier to follow a diagnostic path at the outset than to intervene in a situation of dilemma one cannot control. But the question that arises is: all of us are talking in a moving train and how can a Buddhist blueprint for a confused world be ever implemented? For whatever it is worth, the message has been spelled out from time to time.[35] The socio-economic context in which the Buddha preached was far simpler than ours. He certainly considered poverty and starvation as a kind of crime and a celebrated Jātaka tells how he refused to preach to a hungry man (till he was fed and looked after by his disciples). But during the days of the Buddha the craving for material goods was not so great, people were content with what they had, their wants were fewer and the wealth and income disparities were not as great as they are today. There was less tension, less competition, the population was small and there were no problems with the environment. The Buddha gave simple rules to guide economic activities, which are discussed in a number of *suttas*. For instance, in the *Vygghapajja Sutta* the Buddha outlines three factors which contribute to economic stability and general well-being — production of wealth through skilled and earnest endeavour, its protection, and savings, living within one's means. A guide for simple and contented living could emerge from the innumerable sermons on the subject. The Buddha's principles of economics were not 'neutral' regarding the ends for which people live, an ethical dimension pervaded all aspects of life. This is why after a gap of 2,500 years Schumacher remarked: 'The important question is not our competence regards means but our realism and wisdom regards ends.'

In the economic sphere, the central problem for the Buddha was the satisfaction of man's basic needs which is a necessary prerequisite for his intellectual, moral and spiritual development. By advocating the 'ethic of self-restraint' he showed the way for both the householder and the recluse to lead a simple life. He constructed a balanced lifestyle for them which recommended a modest degree of saving but condemned wastage as well as hoarding and miserliness.

Though there was no integrated concept of distributive justice as such, the idea that the needy should be helped and that wealth should be given to the have-nots was accepted even by the kings. A retiring monarch advises his son in this manner: 'Dear son, and who so ever in thy kingdom are the "have-nots", to them let wealth be given.'[36] A king's economic policy was to be guided by principles of equity. A strong sense of benevolence made the people practice charity and the distribution of goods and wealth (*dāna*) is recommended by the Buddha in place of the sacrifice (*yajña*) recommended in the Brahmanic doctrines.

Concluding thoughts

It has been our aim to make a modest contribution to the discussion of the notion of equality in the Asian religious and cultural traditions, and with this end in view, we have clarified some theoretical strands in the Buddhist perspectives on equality. Studies of this sort could contribute to a deeper, closer and authentic understanding of Asian traditions and encourage students of human rights to undertake in-depth studies of the Eastern and Asian world-view orientations which influence ethico-religious as well as socio-political reflections. The interest in non-Western perspectives on human rights should be encouraged.

It may be premature and even pretentious to suggest any practical line of action. We live in a complex world, and, to cite an example, the question of economic inequality which we considered as our concluding item for discussion is today a gigantic puzzle — it is a vicious circle of food shortages, population growth, inflation, unemployment, overconsumption, social pollution and ideological conflict. However, UNESCO is recommending practical and viable programmes with a strong ethical mission, furthering respect for justice, the rule of law, and the dignity of man without distinctions of race, caste, sex and religion. They function at two levels: they intervene in conflict situations and try to disentangle dilemmas, but they also recommend long-range programmes with a diagnostic focus to change the attitudes of man. If there is a Buddhist contribution to human rights at the practical level, it should be the furtherance of the latter function.[37]

The cross-cultural study of world-views breaks through the temperamental addiction to closed systems, it encourages people to open up their understanding and imagination to probing diverse religious and cultural perspectives and helps them to isolate and preserve all that is of lasting value.[38]

Appendix

Today, the Universal Declaration of Human Rights is considered as 'a common standard of achievement for all people and all nations'. But yet in traditional societies the centrality of human rights varied, and this is seen to be especially true if we study closely the religious and cultural bases of traditional Asian society. Often the life-giving foundations of some of the traditional forms of religion and morality have a slightly different focus, when compared with our concerns for justice, right and wrong and rights which have been given legal and constitutional formulation today.

Peter K.Y. Woo, discussing 'A Metaphysical Approach to Human Rights from a Chinese Point of View' makes the following observations:

> In view of the acceptance of universal unity and harmony, the issue of
> individual rights among men did not take the shape of a problem, nor did

any form of struggling for rights become recognized as a legitimate activity. The role of the ideal of unity awoke the compassionate feelings and the desire for cooperation, rather than the consciousness that the individual needs to be protected.[39]

Sentiments of this sort as voiced by Woo have been occasionally presented in discussions of human rights. But it is rare that a Western scholar penetrates his own culture to discern the shadows of a metaphor of human relationships which is not based on a 'rights-centred morality'. Today many contexts of political and social tensions are presented through the framework of human rights. But we also need a framework which emphasizes not merely competing rights but also conflicting responsibilities.[40] The morality of rights differs from the morality of responsibility; it emphasizes separation rather than connection. But today we need not merely an ethic of rights but also an ethic of care. Such a perspective has been presented in a very interesting study by Gilligan, in her work, *In a Different Voice*:

> In this conception, the moral problem arises from conflicting responsibilities rather than from competing rights and requires for its resolution a mode of thinking that is contextual and narrative rather than formal and abstract. This conception of morality as care centres moral development around the understanding of responsibility and relationships, just as the conception of morality as fairness ties moral development to the understanding of rights and rules.[41]

Gilligan has raised a voice of protest against those who exaggerate the duality between man and woman and thus highlight the dichotomies between the capacity for formal reasoning and autonomous thinking, on the one hand, and the overriding concern with care, love and human relationship, on the other hand — such stereotypic dualities between man and woman appear to point towards a conception of adulthood without a sense of balance and harmony. This perspective may be expanded to engulf wider social and political phenomena which envisage a more comprehensive image of man.

Gilligan discusses her point in relation to an ethical dilemma and possibilities of resolving a situation of conflict which betray a larger tension between two perspectives on morality. A person called Heinz was to decide whether or not he should steal a drug, which he cannot afford to buy, in order to save the life of his wife. Jake, a boy of eleven years, sees the problem in clear logical terms as a conflict between the values of property and the values of life and upholds the priority of life over property. When the same problem is put to an eleven–year–old girl, Amy, it evokes a different type of response: 'Well, I don't think so, I think there might be other ways besides stealing it, like if he should borrow the money or make a loan or something, but he really shouldn't steal the drug — but his wife shouldn't die either.' When a counter-question is asked of Amy as to why the drug should not be stolen, she does not reflect on the value of property or the importance of law, but the effect of the theft on the relationship between Heinz and his wife. The construction of the moral problem in this context as a problem of care and responsibility in relationships rather than rights presents an interesting way of looking at such issues.

Gilligan says that

> The morality of rights is predicated on equality and centered on the understanding of fairness, while the ethic of responsibility relies on the concept of equity, the recognition of differences in need. While the ethic of rights is a manifestation of equal respect, balancing the claims of other and self, the ethic of responsibility rests on an understanding that gives rise to compassion and care. Thus the counterpoint of identity and intimacy that marks the time between childhood and adulthood is articulated through different moralities whose complementarity is the discovery of maturity.[42]

This point of view has been abstracted in the light of her researches into 'images of relationships' between man and woman. Her researches into the feminine psyche place the tension between the ethic of rights and the ethic of care in a new light.

What we wish to emphasize in this brief note is to bring out the idea that, instead of making a one-track concentration on rights, it is necessary to discern other complementary values and ideals which partly generate a tension and partly make our human experience more comprehensive by the integration and reconciliation of conflicting visions regarding man and society. Though the work cited emerged as a contribution to the nature of the feminine psyche, in a deeper psychological sense the duality of these qualities is found in human beings and their complementarity is crucial. It is more than a question of mere gender, but of the nourishment and regeneration of certain human qualities which have been preserved in the evolution of the human race and of qualities which we need without excess and in balance and harmony. In a narrow sense, this duality is derived as a 'metaphor' from the biology and the evolution of man, but this distinction has finer ramifications in social-political life.

5 The Radical Egalitarianism of Mahayana Buddhism

John C. Holt

Social, economic and political equality, in so far as this ideal has been understood in the post-Enlightenment period of the modern West, is not a topic of consideration arising within the context of Mahāyāna Buddhist religious thought. It is clear that Mahāyāna *sūtras* were never intended to function as social charters for hierarchical orders or for egalitarian societies; for these texts are completely innocent of discourses concerned with matters of social theory. Moreover, as a social institution which in various periods of history found favour with state powers in China, Japan, Korea, Tibet and South-East Asia, Mahāyāna did not inspire egalitarian principles that were translated into social policy by political institutions, however progressive these institutions might have been. Wherever Mahāyāna thrived in Asia, it existed within the milieu of hierarchical societies. Some scholars, especially Max Weber,[1] have argued that Buddhist ideas, particularly the cardinal concept of *karma*, have actually had the affect of legitimating social hierarchy. On the other hand, many scholars have recently examined the issue of how Mahāyāna Buddhism has helped to inspire numerous millenarian movements in East Asia which were fundamentally egalitarian, if not radically Utopian, in nature. This chapter, however, is not concerned with these movements[2] nor is it concerned with the eschatology of Maitreya that accompanied them. The basic argument presented herein is that there exists an incipient form of egalitarianism in Mahāyāna which is expressed primarily through metaphysical, psychological and cultural ideals rather than through social values.

Whenever a particular issue or a specific concept is addressed within Mahāyāna Buddhism, it is necessary to determine exactly which aspect of Mahāyāna is the appropriate point of reference. Mahāyāna tradition is by no means a seamless whole and the conditions of its origin(s) are highly obscure. The problem is further complicated by the fact that respective Mahāyāna schools or sects trace their *dharmas* to a wide variety of different *sūtras*, each claiming that their sacred text contains the final authoritative word of the Buddha. For instance, the *Saddhar-*

mapuṇḍarika (Lotus) *Sūtra* was regarded by the Chinese T'ien t'ai (Japanese Tendai) as authoritative, the *Ayatamsaka* was claimed to have the same status for Hua yen (Japanese Kegon) and the *Prajñāpāramita sūtras* were definitive for the Māhyamikas. In addition, Mahāyāna Buddhism was by no means only a scholastic, monastic religious tradition. Similar to the emergent character of *bhakti* traditions of Pūranic Hinduism, Mahāyāna became a thoroughgoing religious devotionalism in popular vicissitudes. As such, it was not heavily invested in, nor very dependent upon, priestly and cultic mediation. That is, it became a religious expression of the common folk as much as it had become an expression of elite, philosophically-orientated minds. Hence, the following discussion is divided into two parts, a division which not only reflects this dual character of Mahāyāna, but also focuses upon the metaphysical principle of central importance to all Mahāyāna schools: *śūnyatā* (emptiness). In the first part, *śūnyatā* is discussed in terms of its evolution as a religious concept in Buddhist tradition; in the second part, the discussion shifts to a consideration of how *śūnyatā* is expressed in religious culture. Herein we find radical expressions of egalitarianism as egalitarianism was understood by Mahāyanā Buddhists. Furthermore, we find these expressions to be avowedly anti-hierarchial.

Śūnyatā in mahāyāna metaphysical idealism

The Sanskrit term *śūnyatā* is derived from the adjective *śūna* translated rudimentally as 'swollen' or 'hollow'. In the formation of compound words, however, the term *śūnya* is usually employed. While retaining its sense of 'hollowness', it usually conveys a meaning of 'vacant' or 'absent'. *Śūnyatā* is a reification of *śūnya* and means 'emptiness' or 'void'. It is especially important to note that these terms do not connote 'absolute nothingness', although this is the sense in which they have often been mistaken, particularly by well-meaning Western commentators. The subtle meaning of *śūnyatā* is difficult to convey to those who are inclined towards a perspective grounded in empiricism or pragmatism. While *śūnyatā* is a descriptive term, it does not, in fact, describe any specific quality. In the Mahàyāna context, it describes 'no-thing'. The difficulty involved in its explanation is partly due to the types of language employed by Indian metaphysicians, partly due to the nature of the arguments involved, and partly due to the fact that *śūnyatā*, when finally grasped, undercuts the very bases of logic and linguistic analysis. One way of tackling this problem is to begin with the manner in which the term was initially employed in Pali canonical literature to identify its meaning as an antecedent concept in Theravāda thought. It is frequently the case that what later gained full fruition in Mahāyāna texts existed inchoate within Theravāda.

Whenever the Buddha is portrayed in debates with rivals from the Brahmanical community or from other heterodox schools, his position is referred to as the 'middle way' between 'eternalism', on the one hand, and 'annihilationism' on the other. Metaphysically, this means that he rejected belief in an enduring, eternal, substantial self or soul which transmigrates from existence to existence while at the same time denying the veracity of fatalistic nihilism. Effectively, the Buddha opposed hedonism and radical forms of asceticism. In formulating his position of 'moderation', he argued that no substantial 'self' (*ātman*) exists. What his Brahmanical opponents took to be a substantial essence is, according to the Buddha, only a conditioned maze of relations which change form over the course of time. Quality and form of being are not only relatively dependent upon already existent phenomena in space and time, but also dependent upon the nature of intention which gives rise to consequential actions. No 'things' can be said to exist autonomously. Being is dependent. The failure to recognize this fundamental fact leads to suffering (*dukkha*), the condition of being due to mistakenly attributing substance to form which in turn leads to desiring after the acquisition of 'things' which are by nature impermanent. As we shall see, *śūnyatā*, as articulated by Nagārjuna some 600 years later, is a radical restatement of the Buddha's view on dependent origination.

Sūnyatā is addressed specifically within the *Majjhimo nikāya* of the Pali canon. Two *suttas*, the *Cūlasuññata* ('Smaller Discourse on Emptiness') and the *Mahāsuññata* ('Greater Discourse on Emptiness') incorporate use of the concept in decidedly varying fashions.[3]

The *Cūlasuññata sutta* consists of a brief homily in which Ānanda has asked the Buddha if he has properly understood what the Buddha really meant when previously he said: 'Abiding in emptiness. I now dwell in the fullness thereof.' Beginning his explanation of this apparently enigmatic statement, the Buddha says that one should carefully attend to perceptions at hand and not be disturbed by anything which is not relevant to immediate perception. That is, perception of a particular object should be empty of any other perceptions. While moderns would praise the Buddha for clearly stating the basic principle of phenomenological inquiry, what the

Buddha was really imparting to Ānanda was a lesson in *vipassana* (insight). He then goes on to illustrate. When one is in the forest, one ought not to be thinking about the village. More to the point, when one is in meditation, one ought to remain in a state of fixed concentration. The discourse then proceeds to a description of how an 'utterly purified perception' is conducive to the realization of the eight ever-rarified planes of consciousness, including the final three: the plane of 'no-thing', the plane of 'neither-perception-nor-non-perception' and finally the last plane which is simply identified as the 'signless'. When one has experienced this highest plane, then one has arrived at a spiritual state which is said to be completely empty of the 'sense pleasures, becoming and ignorance'. Thus 'Abiding in emptiness, I now dwell in the fullness thereof' means developing a mental culture (*bhavana*) that is disciplined in focus and devoid of tendencies of distraction which contribute to the conditioning process. It is concentrated insight into presentational immediacy, a mental mindset conducive to the attainment of the Buddhist spiritual goal.

The *Mahāsuññata sutta* is more explicit. Herein, *suññata* refers to an awareness of the *khandas*, the five conditioned aggregates constitutive of the psycho-physical personality. Essentially, this means awareness of the process that is said to begin with the contact of the sense organs with objects in the phenomenal world finally culminating in consciousness.[4] It was precisely this theory of conditioned being and consciousness that the Buddha used in his debates with rivals who held the 'substantialist/*ātman* position'. 'Self-consciousness' consists of being aware of the process by which mental formations are constructed. This process is considered by the Buddha to be pre-eminently non-substantial and contingent. Awareness of this non-substantial, conditioned and inherently 'empty' process is said to lead to an 'imperturbability' of mind. The Buddha then warns Ānanda that an 'imperturbed' mind does not engage in idle speculation or express itself in relation to matters of a mundane nature. While a perturbed mind expresses hostility in thought and action, an 'imperturbed' mind is calmly disposed and directed towards thoughts of harmlessness and non-grasping. It is imbued with wisdom and inclined to nibbana. Thus, as the *Cūlasuññata* characterizes 'abiding in emptiness' as an undistracted, concentrated experience of insight, the *Mahāsuññata* sees it an awareness of emptiness that fosters evenmindedness. In the former, emptiness is the absence of distractions; in the latter, it is a cultivated awareness of the non-substantial process of knowing and being.

Whereas these two Pali *suttas* are explicitly concerned with the psychological processes involved with meditation and self-awareness, a later Hinayāna school, the Sautrāntikas, analysed dependent origination in metaphysical terms. As the Buddha had maintained in the *Cūlasuññata sutta* that one should fully concentrate upon the contemporaneous occasion, the Sautrāntikas analysed the nature of these occasions *per se*. Asserting that subjective consciousness was continuous, the Sautrāntikas argued that occasions of cognition were composed of an infinite number of successive *dharmas* or moments. Each *dharma* uprises and fades only to be succeeded by another. Even though dharmas are sequential, they never overlap. They do not form a flowing continuity. Rather, they are almost cinematographic in nature. Furthermore, a previous occasion or *dharma* does 'not act' upon its successor. Its presence only sets the context for what follows. Each moment is novel or 'contained'. For example, a Sautrāntika would say: 'The tree I now behold is not the same tree that I was beholding a moment ago; nor, for that matter, am I the same person beholding it.' Despite this, he would maintain that there is a continuous relation between objective *dharmas* and their subjective realizations. A *dharma* is what it is 'in its own time' even though it is objectively and subjectively dependent. Thus, the Sautrāntika metaphysical description of *dharma* would seem to be fully consistent with the basis of the Buddha's advice to Ānanda in the *Cūlasuññata*.

The Mahāyāna understanding of *śūnyatā*, as it was articulated by Nagārjuna, commences at the point where the Sautrāntikas left off and seems to incorporate the views of the *Mahāsuññata* as well. The Sautrāntikas did not attempt to analyse the relationship between *dharmas* of successive occasions and remained content with a kind of positive, phenomenological nominalism. Nagārjuna, however, made this issue the centre of his discussion regarding emptiness. If each *dharma* is impermanent due to the fact that it uprises and fades, yet prepares the ground for *dharmas* to follow, the relationship existing between successive *dharmas* would seem to imply a 'real' ground between them. But, by asserting that a 'real' ground exists between *dharmas*, and by describing this ground positively, Nagārjuna would run the risk of positing substance objectively and 'self' subjectively. That is, by admitting to the positive reality of a 'ground of being', Nagārjuna's argument could be construed as the 'eternalist' position or the claim that an *ātman* exists in the stream of consciousness. Unprepared to argue the existence of either a 'ground of being' or a 'self', Nagārjuna took the bold opposite track. His revolutionary argument is as follows: if being is constituted by relations (which is the fundamental argument of dependent origination), then all being is absolutely empty. What exists between *dharmas* (that is, relations) is emptiness. Since consciousness exists through the process of dependent origination, it is also fundamentally empty. It follows that all mental constructions, which are the product of consciousness, are therefore empty. This basic fact, he argued, holds as much for the simplest sentence as it does for the Four Noble Truths. Nagārjuna went so far as to admit that even the concept of emptiness is empty. The consequences of Nagārjuna's argument for cosmology and soteriology were equally prodigious. Since nirvana is the state of the unfettered 'no-relation', and if *saṃsāra* consists of relations which in reality are empty, both can be equated. Ultimately and absolutely, both *saṃsāra* and nirvana are empty and cannot be delineated or differentiated. What Nagārjuna had done was to undercut the commonsense understanding of differentiation, hierarchy, individuality and plurality. His radical restatement of Buddhist ontology, which became normative for Mahāyāna speculative idealism from Madhyāmika to Zen, is simply stated in the earlier *Prajñāpāramita sùtras* in the following verse:

Form is emptiness;
Emptiness is form.

Alternatively, one can say: 'No-things exist', or 'all things are empty'.

What this Mahāyāna Buddhist had come to understand is that reason and language cannot adequately express the true facts about reality. Nagārjuna's position is one that maintains that although reality can be experienced and known, it cannot be fully known or experienced in convention.

Nagārjuna's argument undercuts commonsense distinctions made subjectively and the reality of differentiation in the objective sphere. However, the fact remains that identifications of particular objects in phenomenal existence continue to be made, individuation occurs, and multiplicity is encountered in every day existence. While Nagārjuna had argued that these identifications, individuations and multiplicity are ultimately false, he left room in his argument for the veracity of their relative condition. This was accomplished by Nagārjuna and later Mahāyāna thinkers through the incorporation of the 'doctrine of two truths'. From a conditioned perspective, or from a point of view anchored to some referent, one does make distinctions. And these distinctions are relatively true within a context. For a perspective that is qualified makes qualified distinctions. This is known as the truth of *samvṛti*, or the truth of things compounded. But, there also exists *Pāramartha*, or absolute truth, which is not anchored in any point of reference and is the perspective of truth understood from the vantage of *śūnyatā*. The truth of *Pāramartha* is utterly unarisen, uncompounded, and unconditioned. It is the nature of existence *per se: bhūtathata* — suchness, thusness, thatness. The doctrine of two truths is more readily understood than *śūnyatā*. In the world of common sense, relative judgements are made on the basis of regarding 'things' as substantial and distinctions as definitive. These 'things' are given labels or names, categories are hierarchized, and conventions are agreed upon in order to facilitate communication and the business of every day life. But from a non-perspective (or beyond a particular conditioned perspective), things are actually what they are in their own suchness and remain just that in spite of the refracting lenses of conditioned perspectives. If it were possible to be abstracted from a given location to view all of the world and its events simultaneously, one could understand that existence is a seamless whole moving through the course of time. That is, from the perspective of the unconditioned absolute, existence is really just one-related-being, the realization of which is *Pāramartha*. *Bhūtathata* is actually a positive way of stating *śūnyatā*.

Despite the relative clarity that the doctrine of the two truths brings to the notion of *śūnyatā*, interpreters of Mahāyāna have continued to struggle with the concept. For example, Suzuki stated that *śūnyatā* 'simply means conditioning or the transitoriness of all phenomenal existences'.[6] He seems to have better described the truth of *samvṛti* than the truth of *Pāramartha*. Stcherbatsky seems to have taken the same track when he translated *śūnyatā* as 'relativity': 'We use the term relative to express the fact that a thing can be identified only by mentioning its relations to something else, and becomes meaningless without these relations'.[7] Both Suzuki and Stcherbatsky, in their apparent eagerness to avoid the misconception that *śūnyatā* should not be equated with nothingness, have left the truth of *Pāramartha* out of the absolute/relative equation of *śūnyatā*.

There is no doubt that early Mahāyāna thinkers also struggled with *śūnyatā*. One later group of Mahāyānists, the Yogācārins, abandoned the emphasis on metaphysics and returned the discussion of *śūnyatā* to the psychological level from whence its consideration had originally commenced in the Pali *suttas*.

The Yogācārins were known as the 'mind-only' school because in their version of subjective idealism, they attributed all objects in the phenomenal world to projections of the mind and then went on to equate *śūnyatā* with the mind in its unfettered state. While it is true that they incorporated the metaphysical idealism of Nagārjuna into their speculations, they were also concerned with very fundamental and practical questions such as how we make errors in judgement and what accounts for memory and its processes.

The Yogācārins, whose influence is seen very clearly in the subsequent evolution of Ch'an and Zen in China and Japan, also took the teachings of the Sautrāntikas as their point of departure. But instead of referring to the continuous uprising and passing away of *dharmas* in the sequential process of consciouness, the Yogācārins asserted that the mind 'stored' past impressions derived from karmic experience in the form of 'seeds' which 'ripened' to fruition when stimulated in existential encounters. The maturations of these 'seeds' is what produced mental images of objects in the phenomenal world and what accounts for the experience of recognition and memory. The mind itself, however, is like a mirror or a screen upon which these activated images dance. The images are contingent, but the mind is not, although in absolute truth the two cannot be differentiated. A passage from *The Awakening of Faith* clearly illustrates the relation between the mind and its projections:

> Water can be said to be identical and not–identical with waves. Waves are stirred up by the wind, but the water remains the same. When the wind ceases, the motion of the water subsides; but the water remains the same. Likewise, when the mind of all religious creatures which in its own nature is pure and clean is stirred up by the wind of ignorance, the waves of mentality make their appearance. Neither the mind nor ignorance has any form and attribute of its own. They condition each other. But the mind itself, not being the principle of disturbance, has its movability cease when ignorance is gone. In essence, wisdom remains unmolested.[8]

The 'unmolested' nature of the mind in its original state is called the *alaya-vijñāna*, the 'store-house of consciousness'. It is similar to the unconscious known to modern Western psychology. It contains the 'seeds' functioning as the potential sources of mental formations, memory patterns, and so on. In short, it contains the potential for the structure of mental existence. If it is agitated, or becomes 'anxious' through sense contact with the phenomenal world, these 'stored seeds' ripen to fruition. But a person gradually progressing towards enlightenment is slowly eliminating 'seeds' which are defiling by nature. In the *sūtras* of the Yogācāra school (*Lankāyatara, Srīmāla-devisimhanāda,* and so on), the 'store-house of consciousness', pure in its unagitated state of potential, was equated with *śūnyatā* and *Tathāgatagarbha*. *Tathāgatagarbha* is a Sanskrit compound. The meaning of *garbha* is 'womb', 'inner room', 'embryo', 'the calyx of a lotus'. The *Tathagata* refers to the Buddha as 'the one-who-has-thus-come'.[9] Thus the mind in its unfettered state is here equated with the 'embryo of the Buddha' or as 'Buddha-nature' as it was later known. The Prajñāpāramitas had previously made use of a uteral metaphor when they alluded to the perfection of wisdom as a goddess and the 'mother of all Buddhas'. But the Yogācārins took the matter one step further; by equating *Tathāgatagarbha* with *alaya-vijñāna*, they were making the claim that within every person there exists the potential of becoming a Buddha.[10] By extension, *tathata*, 'suchness', is innate in all sentient beings.

In this overview of the evolution of the concept of *śūnyatā*, what has emerged is one long, massive equation: *Pratītyasamutpāda* (dependent origination) = *śūnyatā* = *tathata* = *alaya* = *vijñāna* = *Tathāgatagarbha* (Buddha-nature) = mind. As is quite evident, this equation can have a great 'leveling' effect. It is to the practical religious expressions of this equation that we now turn our attention.

Emptiness and practical expressions of egalitarianism

In the history of religions, it is often difficult to ascertain whether or not major transformations in religious thought are responses to social change or are a key factor in the promotion of social change. The problem is more acute in the context of the history of Indian religions due to the abundance of religious literature and the paucity of corroborating historical data. It is probably safe to say that the relation between socio-historical reality and religious thought is reflexive in nature. Therefore, when the changes in the Mahāyāna conception of the bodhisattva are addressed in the next few pages, it is likely that alterations in this ideal reflected corresponding changes in the role itself.

The metaphysical and psychological centrality of *śūnyatā* and *alaya-vijñāna* respectively reflect revolutionary changes in the Buddhist tradition, especially after these notions became allied with Taoist notions of a kindred nature in the Chinese context. Foremost among these changes was the positive valorization of *samsāra*. Nagārjuna's assertions regarding emptiness, the doctrine of two truths and the universalism of *alaya-vijñāna* combined with the Chinese understanding of Tao to produce a monistic view of the cosmos. Nowhere is this monistic perspective as clearly evident as in the teachings of Chinese Hua Yen (Yogācārin). For in Hua Yen, not only was every being endowed with *Tathāgatagarbha*, but all *dharmas* were understood to interpenetrate one another. Hua Yen, which for many comprised the philosophy of Ch'an, was fond of the use of metaphors to explain the interpenetration of all 'things'. And in the extrapolation of these metaphors we see reflected important implications for the Bodhisattva ideal and role. 'The Jewel Net of Indra' and the 'rafter and the barn' are two such metaphors.

'The Jewel Net of Indra' is connected at every intersection of its strands by a pure jewel (the mind) which in its sheer lucidity reflects the brilliance of all other gems. That is, in one's own 'diamond mind' is reflected the totality of all other minds. But, by cutting loose even one of the gems, of the cosmic lace, the entire net unravels and it ceases to be what it was before. Thus, in one mind lies the possibility of all minds. The meaning of the metaphor of the rafter and the barn is similar. Can the rafter and the barn be separated? In the rafter lies the possibility of the barn. And if one removes the rafter, the barn collapses. In the part, the possibility of the whole is contained.

This line of thought has major implications for the Bodhisattva ideal. In the first instance, since all sentient beings are endowed with Buddha-nature and emptiness is the character of all relations between entities, hierarchy and duality are absolutely banished. If Mahāyāna had its origins, in part, in a more liberal understanding of the path of the Buddhist holy man, which would seem to be the case given the arguments of the Second Great Buddhist Council, then one can readily see how the evolution of Mahāyāna thought legitimated an even more liberal understanding in later times and in other cultural contexts. If distinctions between *samsāra* and nirvana were ultimately empty, if the part could not be separated from the whole, and if every living being was endowed with Buddha-nature, on what basis could distinctions between householder and monk, male and female, rich and poor, he made legitimate? In fact, when we consider the evolving conception of the Bodhisattva, we see that they were demolished in the minds of many Mahāyāna adherents.

The *Vimilakīrti-Nirdesa Sūtra* contains a vivid portrayal of the radical egalitarianism which surfaces in Mahāyāna: Vimilakīrti is a layman who has realized the truth of emptiness. His wisdom is so vast and superior that he succeeds in defeating all of the celestial Bodhisattvas in debate. He proceeds to preach *dharma* to each of them until he meets his equal in Manjūśri. In comparison to Vimilakīrti, the narrowness of the Theravāda arhats is ridiculed. In his sermons, he preaches that even the worst sinners still have a chance to achieve nirvana. Uimilakīrti then makes the vow that until each of them is assured this attainment and thereby realeased from the condition of suffering, he will not attain the final nirvana himself. In this late Indian Mahāyāna *sūtra*, we can see a popularization of the principles of *śūnyatā*, *alaya-vijñāna* and interpenetration of all *dharmas* at work. The distinction between monk and layman, moreover, the distinction between layman and Bodhisattva, has even been satirized. Spiritual attainment does not depend upon a hierarchical status, but on insight into the true nature of reality. But more importantly — and here is the key — since Uimilakīrti knows that ultimately his own being is related even to the worst of sinners, he also knows that in their salvation lies his own. *Śūnyatā* necessarily implies that the path of action of a Bodhisattva consists of selflessness, a striving for the spiritual attainment of the entire cosmos.

Transcending the distinctions intrinsic to the world of *samvṛti* (the truth of things compounded), the Bodhisattva, in order to toil self-lessly for the salvation of all, is not ridden by the dualities of male and female, pure and impure, and so on. Throughout his efforts, he remains 'uncontaminated' and unrestrained in his selfless effort and knowledge of the oneness of existence. This is graphically illustrated not only in stories about Avalokiteśvara, who wanders through the hells to bring the *dharma* to the dammed, but also in *Vajrayāna* rites of sexual intercourse. Not only does the Bodhisattva refuse to separate his own salvation from all others, but the phenomenal world of samsaric existence becomes a stage for him to act upon. Thus, *samsāra* is not a realm from which one is to be set free or a realm to flee from, but it is pre-eminently the world to act within. Impurity does not result from association with the impure, but from ignorance and a defiled mind. In the same manner that Nagārjuna is said to have 'negated the negation' of dialectical thought by undermining its very principle through propounding the truth of *śūnyatā*, so the Bodhisattva negates the negative condition of *samsāra* which arises due to the perception of duality between *samsāra* and nirvana. This Mahāyāna truth is radically expressed by the eighteenth–century Japanese Zen monk Hakuin for whom even urine and dung are considered as expressions of Buddha-nature.

While this radical egalitarian ethos would seem to provide a fertile ground for the implanting of the social values of equality such as equality of opportunity, the uplifting of the status of women, and the demolition of privileged positions amongst the aristocracy, its influence did not seem to follow this course. While many principles of Mahāyāna idealism and religious practice became secularized, impact was made directly or in diffused fashion in the cultural rather than in the social sphere. The expression of Mahāyāna radical egalitarianism is found most clearly in the Ch'an and Zen traditions.

It has been said that in order to study and practice Zen, one must have a general 'house-cleaning' of the mind. This is because, as Nagārjuna and the Yogācārins have shown, idealistic constructions and language are fundamentally empty and the mind in its original state (*alaya-vijñāna*) is pure. Consequently, there has developed in Zen both an iconoclastic and an anti-intellectual attitude. One well-known contemporary Zen *roshi* has put the matter this way: 'In the beginner's mind, there are many possibilities, but in the expert's there are few.'[12] In Zen traditions, there is great love for the entirely simple and the basically unconfused, a love cultivated through a variety of spiritual exercises and cultural expressions. This love for simplicity is illustrated in the lives of numerous, eminent monks who are regarded as outstanding figures in the history of the tradition.

Hui Nēng, the Sixth Patriarch in line from Bodhidharma in a spiritual geneology which traces itself back to Nagārjuna and ultimately to Sakyamuni, was an illiterate and orphaned firewood cutter and rice pounder when he composed a poem that won him the right to succeed the Fifth patriarch, Hung-jēn. At the time, the foremost of Hung-jēn's disciples had been Shen-hsiu. In the view of all of his peers, Shen-hsiu deserved to succeed Hung-jēn. To demonstrate his worthiness to succeed Hung-jēn, Shen-hsiu wrote the following verse on the pillared hall of the monastery late one night:

> The body is the Bodhi tree,
> The mind is like a clear mirror standing.
> Take care to wipe it all the time,
> Allow no grain of dust to cling.

The following morning, all of the monks gathered around the *gātha*, admired it, and thought that the question of succesion had now been settled. In their presence, Hung-jēn praised the verse but privately he told Shen-hsiu that the poem showed little understanding of enlightenment and that he should try once again. The young Hui-nēng, who could neither read nor write, had the poem recited to him twice. Late that night, he had a second verse written (audaciously) on the wall which read:

> The body is not like a tree,
> The clear mind is nowhere standing.
> Fundamentally, not one thing exists;
> Where, then, is a grain of dust to cling?

This poem also won the immediate approval of the monks, although they could scarcely guess its source. But Hung-jēn was very reserved and erased the lines, saying that its author had not yet gained enlightenment. But secretly that night, he summoned Hui-nēng to his room and conferred the patriarchship upon him.[13]

This legend, which might have originated to depict subsequent schism over sudden and gradual enlightenment between southern and northern schools of Ch'an in seventh-century China, is highly indicative of the simplicity and clarity of Zen while at the same time showing Zen's affection for ordinariness and innocence.

Just as Indian Mahāyāna metaphysics and the evolution of the Bodhisattva ideal had culminated in the positive valorization of samsāra, Zen valorized such mundane tasks as sweeping, kitchen duty and gardening. These actions were held to be as valuable as any other. The form of a task was of no importance, rather it was the way in which a task was carried out with right intention and mindfulness. This ethic is portable and became a principle in such diverse activities as painting, poetry, the tea ceremony, archery and swordsmanship. For Zen, there is no dichotomy between thought and action. Zen is the negation of Cartesian perspectives. In its expressions, the mind reflects the suchness of existence. The sword is not external to the swordsman. It should move as an extension, as an intrinsic part of the mind. The same should be true of the pen and paint brush. What is most important is the spontaneous expression of the disciplined, enlightened mind in utter simplicity. Much of the practice of Zen essentially involves recovering the original unfettered nature of the mind. And this can be accomplished in virtually any context. Hence the valorization of all action. Nature and children are particularly singled out as examples of simplicity, spontaneity and ordinariness. As Basho wrote:

> 'I do not like children.'
> For him who says this
> No flowers bloom.

Conclusion

The ethos of Zen in particular and Mahāyāna in general is radically egalitarian and anti-hierarchical. Yet, however much this ethos is illustrated, the fact of the matter is that even Zen has been put into the service of protecting hierarchy. That is, Zen techniques developed to cultivate a disciplined, even-minded mental disposition were put to effective use by late medieval feudal lords in Japan in order to train their armies. In other words, even-mindedness can be put to use in the quest for political power in pyramidal societal structures. Perhaps that is one price paid for such a 'portable' ethic.

Moreover, in considering the radical egalitarianism of Mahāyāna Buddhism, one is struck by the fact that its clearest expressions and its ultimate realizations occur on the level of the individual (mind) and on the level of the universal (cosmos). At the level of society, however, it does not seem to be evident at all. Even within the context of the monastic institution in China and Japan, hierarchy seems to have become a necessity.

The problem regarding equality in Mahāyāna Buddhism seems to lie with the very manner in which equality can be defined. For Mahāyāna, egalitarianism does not seem to have meant the social equality of one individual *vis-à-vis* another. An individual's social identity, duties of obligation and his rights to behave in certain ways were determined by the *dharmas* of caste and station in life in India and role within the family context in China. These powerful social conventions are rooted in hierarchical conceptions, conceptions that are not focused upon the individual or the cosmos but upon society *per se*.

It has recently been suggested that the spontaneity and licence found in the popular cults of bhakti tradition, especially in the Vaiṣṇava Kṛṣṇa cult of the Braj district in northern India, may represent a reaction to the rigidly structured conventions of social *dharma*.[14] That is, religious thoughts and behaviour can be interpreted as 'releases' from normative social constraints. There may be some validity in applying this thesis to Mahāyāna. It is well known, for instance, that Mahāyāna was persecuted in various periods of Chinese history precisely because it was perceived as a threat to the basic family structure. Mahāyāna apologists frequently had to argue that Mahāyāna posed no such threat. And it is also well known that the basic Brahmanical criticism of early Buddhism was that it was a threat to family and caste. These persecutions and criticisms may in fact be reactionary responses to what was perceived accurately as a radical egalitarian spirit.

It is often the case that those holding the reins of political power attempt to enlist the teaching of religions to legitimate the hierarchies in which they find themselves at the apex. When religion is bastardized in this fashion, this is done not for religious purposes but for political ends. It follows, then, that if Mahāyāna was put to use by political powers to legitimate hierarchy, Mahāyāna need not be equated with hierarchy *per se*. That there were Mahāyānists who recognized this truth is illustrated in a metaphysical discussion elaborated upon by Ts'ao-shan of the Ts'aotung (Japanese Soto) sect in ninth-century China. The discussion, predictably, is concerned with the relationship between the absolute and the relative or phenomenal. This was a discussion of the so-called 'Five Ranks', a teaching rooted in *Prajñāpāramita* but shaped in accordance with the principles of the *I Ching* (Book of Changes). The 'Five Ranks' are said to develop as follows:

1. The Absolute is within the relative — because the Absolute merges completely with the relative, the 'knower' gives up pondering the absolute and plunges himself entirely into phenomenal existence; thus, since the movement is from Absolute to relative, the first rank is symbolized as follows: ◕
2. The relative with the Absolute — because the relative is imbued with the Absolute, one abandons the relative and enters the Absolute; since the movement is from relative to Absolute, the second rank is symbolized as follows: ◔
3. The Absolute alone — because the relative exists potentially in the Absolute, one contemplates its 'seeds'; since the Absolute contains the possibility of the relative, it is symbolized as follows: ○
4. The relative alone — because contemplation of relative forms in their solitariness makes the absolute apparent, the fourth rank is symbolized as follows: ○

Whereas the first two 'ranks' suggest the interpenetration of the relative and the absolute, the third and fourth signify that the relative and the absolute are apparent in each other. The fifth and highest rank signifies their undifferentiated oneness:

5. The Absolute and the relative together because the Absolute and the relative are one and thus negate all opposites, and because the

fifth rank is the realization of enlightenment, it is symbolized as follows: ●

Now, the famous commentary on the 'Five Ranks' was written by Ts'ao-shan. It is a very simple piece making use of a single occasion in the experience of social hierarchy to illustrate the profound egalitarianism of Mahāyāna Buddhism:

1. The lord sees the vassal.
2. The vassal turns toward the lord.
3. The lord (alone).
4. The vassal (alone).
5. The lord and vassal in union.[15]

6 Conceptions of Equality and Human Nature in Taoism

Yoshimi Murakami

Introduction

Correction of the inequality prevalent in the societies of the modern world is frequently sought by means of various socialist conceptions as well as through the organization of the United Nations and the like. Yet all these measures are being applied from the outside, and thus true equality is not easily to be achieved. Parallel to these efforts, we must think of human equality as being realized within each and every individual. In order to do so we have to consider the question of man's actual character, that is, what human nature is in fact like.

I have entitled this chapter 'Conceptions of Equality and Human Nature in Taoism', but the concept of equality in Taoism is very different from what is believed to be equality nowadays in terms of 'rights'. Similarly, the Taoist idea of human nature is not like Kant's reason or the self as understood in English utilitarianism. The concept of human nature in Taoism is based on its notion of the source of the universe, of Tao, from which all existence, men as well as the world of nature, spring forth and draw their life. Only inasmuch as man is connected with this spring of universal life, with the Tao, can he ever realize his true inner nature. For this reason, human nature in Taoism is closely linked to life as such, and the source of this life is apparent in desire.

Man's desire knows no limit, and gradually it tends to become corrupt and a force of destruction. Then the situation described by Thomas Hobbes as *'bellum omnium contra omnes'* is reached. On the other hand, the total elimination of all desire can only mean death. Between these two extremes, religions, philosophies and ethical systems all over the world have searched for ways of limiting desire. Though they have come up with widely different methods to do so, in their basic aim their efforts are identical. And the classical economic philosophy of Adam Smith as well as the communist system of Marx are very similar in their basic attempt to limit desire.

However, Taoism does not actually attempt to limit human desire, it rather sets out to purify or spiritualize it. Just as one purifies the muddy water of the Yellow River and transforms it into drinking water, one purifies human desire, and the more one advances in this purification, the more beneficial desire is bound to become. Ever since antiquity, economic development has gone hand in hand with scientific progress and technological advance, but all progress and development have always been solidly based on human desire. Likewise, all human culture, art, religion and philosophy have invariably been kindled by the flame of man's desire. Thus desire can be said to be the sprout of all culture, the seed of all life.

It is in this sense that Taoism conceived of desire as of central importance, and of the purification of desire as a means to the attainment of longevity and immortality (*pu-lao ch'ang-sheng*). The desire for long life gave rise to medicine, herbology, alchemy and various other sciences, but it was mainly aimed at a mystical union with the underlying principles of the universe, the Tao. This was accomplished by breathing in the never ending life of the Tao, by purifying one's earthly desires. Mystical union with the Tao implied going all the way to a state of no-mind (*wu-hsin*), to the complete negation of a personal self, but once unification with the Tao was realized, eternal life energy was obtained. The way there was conceived in very practical and technical terms, the final goal as the birth of the self, of the true self.

The notion of the spiritualization, the purification of desire, is firmly embedded in the Taoist concept of human nature, yet its validity is not limited to Taoism alone, but can also be applied to humankind at large. This is because spiritualization of desire means liberation of human nature, and only on the basis of a liberated nature can man's inner equality be established. This in turn is the only thinkable and valid foundation for true equality among mankind.

Conception of equality

How inequality was created

Human beings have suffered great harm that comes out of various conflicts, especially those which appear among religious groups. These conflicts have seriously injured us by creating many kinds of inequality. Even now, this problem remains unsolved: all the religions of the world are still unable to remove inequality from our society. Irrationally enough, we are always deeply divided by religious conflicts, although all religions were founded with an aim to establish peace among us. Nevertheless, I believe, we can discover the key to resolving this dilemma in seeking some ideas common to all religions. The way we have to follow is, needless to say, extremely difficult, and yet significant.

First of all, we have to know on what basic foundation all religions are built. In my view, a religion originates in one's emotional states, especially in a state of serious discouragement. Such a state of mind is named '*Scheitern*' by philosophers. Without exception, the greatest religions began with the direct experience of *Scheitern*, though now they have established a highly-developed system of thought, as seen in their views of God, the world and life. The experience of *Scheitern* compels us to consider how we are made: it brings us a new point of view, through which we can recognize the world as a whole. When it brings us to its extremity, we discover the presence of the Absolute in ourselves: a seed of belief is planted in our heart. As I said above, there are various religions in the world, and many conflicts among them are not easily resolved. Nevertheless, once we have recognized that all religions are founded upon the emotional state common to all individuals, we realize one another's agony, sharing the painful experiences of *Scheitern*.

Human existence and equality

The philosophy of existentialism is founded upon an idea similar to Taoist philosophy. Jaspers defines the human experience of *Scheitern* as a foundation on which the philosophical structure of existentialism is built: when we are seriously discouraged, we are forced to doubt the existence of all, and at last to count all for nothing. Jaspers' definition shows clearly that the philosophy of existentialism has based its structure upon the concept of nothingness.

In the oriental world, also, there is a great tradition of the negative philosophy founded by Lao-tzu and Chuang-tzu. This tradition reaches its summit at the time of Kuo Hsiang,[1] the philosopher of the Six Dynasties, whom we shall discuss later. Lao-tzu's view of human nature should be examined first. Chapter 30 of *Lao-tzu*[2] says:

> But when all are joyous as if celebrating the Great Sacrifice or climbing the heights in spring, then I alone — so passive — giving no sign, like an infant

that has not yet smiled; — so forlorn — like one who has nowhere to turn!
When all men have plenty, I alone am like one who is left out.
    I have indeed the heart of a fool — so obtuse!
    Let ordinary men be bright and intelligent, I alone am stupid and confused.
    Let ordinary men be astute and far-sighted, I alone am dull and mope-eyed.
    Wan like the waning moon; adrift like one who has nowhere to rest!
    Let all men have a purpose, I alone am ignorant like a boor.
    I alone am different from others because I prize feeding on 'the Mother'.

As seen in the quoted passage, the speaker regards himself as a passive, forlorn, left-out, foolish and obtuse being: he is alone and completely isolated from everything. His expression is full of agony and uneasiness. Furthermore, the subject 'I' is often used in this chapter. This is an exceptional case in *Lao-tzu*. This shows that the speaker's subjective consciousness is strongly emphasized in this passage.

Such an existential view of human nature forms a foundation of Taoist equalitarianism, which is characteristically seen in the philosophy of Lao-tzu. Let us examine Chapter 56 of his book:

He stops his apertures, he closes his doors.
He blunts sharpness, he unravels tangles,
he dims brightness, he levels tracks.
This is called the mystic equality — Therefore the most prized in All-under-heaven.

This passage shows that the Taoist ideal society is to be constructed under the assumption that a virtuous philosopher is the best king. Although public security and happiness depend on the presence of a sage ruler, he stays at the lowest level of society in order to hide his true identity. This way of reigning makes it possible for him to live on the same rank as his people. The equality between the ruler and his people is thus established. Taoists call such a way of king's rule 'mystic equality'.

Modern western philosophy and Taoism

Three characteristic philosophies of the modern Western world, English utilitarianism, German idealism and French equalitarianism, have afforded basic ideas to modern democracy. German idealism is represented by Kant, and in his philosophy the concept of human dignity is especially emphasized. Kant shows man's *'innere Würde'* being realized by denying all restrictions except his own reason. The concept of *innere Würde* is the origin from which he deduced the idea of autonomous freedom. In his philosophy reason is defined as the essence of human existence, as '*das eigentliche Selbst*'. In an ideal society, or as he names it, '*Reich der Zwecke*', each individual aims at the perfection of his self, and in so doing the true equality of society is realized. Although a modern democratic society reflects such a Kantian view, we can hardly say that it attains his ideal society: we are likely to claim our own personal rights, and human dignity is easily ignored. Thus arises egoism, discouraging us to look sympathetically at others' situations. Why is such a sorrowful state produced? The main reason is that the movements of enlightenment have attempted to distribute equally society's property and powers by overthrowing the traditional notions which were the basis of the former order. In these attempts many admirable traditions have been broken down, and human beings were compelled to make themselves 'smaller'. Nietzsche was indignant at the vices prevailing in modernization movements, and made a negative judgement on modern democracy. Instead, he dreamed of an ideal society composed of *Übermenschen*'. He attempted to establish an absolutely affirmative vision through his nihilistic experiences. As often pointed out, Nietzsche absorbed the spirit of oriental philosophy through Schopenhauer, whom he had once respected. Therefore emphasis should be placed on some of his ideas, which are similar to Taoist philosophy. Likewise, oriental philosophy has greatly influenced the strain of existential thought which famous philosophers such as Jaspers, Heidegger and Sartre bequeathed. Although Jaspers,[3] Heidegger, and Max Weber[4] placed themselves in the great tradition of Western philosophy, they were also deeply impressed by oriental ideas, especially by ideas seen in the Lao–Chuang philosophy. As I showed above, the concept of nothingness affords a foundation to existential philosophy: existentialists attempt to acquire an absolute affirmative view through their negative experiences. This shows clearly their familiarity with Taoist philosophy.

The great river Hwang Ho and Taoism

The idea of social inequality derives from a struggle for existence. Chinese civilization began with the annual floods of the River Hwang Ho, the Yellow River. In ancient days people were compelled to make concerted efforts in subduing the river's floods, and therefore a powerful leadership was essential, and this was required also for the organization of irrigation works. Thus we can conclude that the characteristic geographical circumstances of China offered a favourable environment to produce a powerful despotic monarchy. As Max Weber and Wittfogel have already pointed out, the origin of Chinese despotic monarchies were closely related with the Yellow River's water.

Against powerful princes, Lao-tzu and Chuang-tzu produced their philosophic systems. Taoist philosophy originated in the class of common people, and, in one view, developed itself as a tactical way of resistance against powerful despotic monarchies. It is very noteworthy that Lao-tzu and Chuang-tzu were also inspired by water. The philosophy they built up had its origin in the culture of the Yin ages. It is supposed that both Lao-tzu and Chuang-tzu came of ruined noble lines whose fathers had once belonged to the Yin dynasty. When the monarchy of Yin was replaced by the Chuo kings, most of its ruined people were enslaved and the rest of them came to be engaged in the peddling business. At that time the weakest and most suppressed people in Chinese society were represented by slaves and peddlers. This shows that Taoist philosophy was once a tactical way to fight aginst power holders. In other words, the weakest acquired a general truth that the soft can be consequently superior to the hard. They learned it from their long and painful experiences as well as their own contemplation of water. They were inspired by the vitality and fluid stability of the great River Hwang Ho.

Equalization by water

Of the many properties of water, the capability to abolish every discrimination is the most characteristic one. The weakest are able to equalize themselves with the strongest by utilizing this capability of water. The philosophy of Lao-tzu and Chuang-tzu, which is essentially inspired by water, shows us how the poor and common people can oppose the power-holders' violence. Although their teaching was born in ancient times, it still remains a precious wisdom for us, because even today we observe many people oppressed severely in several countries. It is a well-known fact that class strife among Warring States existed in a particular historical context, and greatly influenced the teaching of Lao-tzu and Chuang-tzu. Indeed this teaching is inseparable from the idea of a class strife, though the book of Lao-tzu, in some phrases, clearly recommends the renunciation of weapons. In this point it bears some resemblance to Mo-tu's philosophy, which mainly discusses how to keep a nation warless by making enough preparations for defence against any invaders. Chapter 76 of *Lao-tzu* says:

> Man at birth is soft and weak, at death he is hard and rigid.
> The ten thousand things, plants and trees, while alive, are soft and fragile; at their death they are dry and withered.
> For, what is hard and rigid is a follower of death; what is soft and weak is a follower of life.
> Therefore, if a weapon is too rigid, it is destroyed; if a tree is too rigid, it breaks. What is hard and rigid is placed below; what is soft and weak is placed above.

In these passages *Lao-tzu* emphasizes the softness of the young in contrast with the hardness of the aged. The softness of the young is closely related with the nature of water: their softness is produced by the water that they contain in themselves. On the contrary, the lack of water as seen in the aged person makes him very stiff, not only at the physical level but at the intellectual. Therefore, generally speaking, old men are stubborn and rigorous, while young men are quick-minded and flexible. Chapter 78 of *Lao-tzu* shows that what is soft and fragile is vital as well as aggressive:

> There is in all the world nothing that is softer or weaker than water, but in attacking what is hard and strong, nothing surpasses it. The weak conquers the strong and the soft conquers the hard. Though every one in the world knows this, no one is able to practice it.

Here *Lao-tzu* shows that the hard and strong is easily conquered by the soft and weak, whose nature is properly exemplified by water. Let us examine Chapter 8:

> The highest goodness is like water. The goodness of water consists in benefiting the ten thousand things without even striving. It stays in the (lowest) place which all men loathe. Therefore it comes near to the Way.

What is discussed here is that water is not less than the very matrix from which all life springs; and that water competes with nothing until it streams its way down to the lowest level. *Lao-tzu* emphasizes that the aggressive nature of water comes from its softness and flexibility. This is an essence of Taoism which has come to function as a tactical principle against powerful rulers.

The ideal King

Lao-tzu profoundly contemplated nature[5] itself and in so doing could find out a significant philosophical meaning. Before our eyes, nature unfolds itself as an exemplified emblem or *Tao*, the very basic element of the Cosmos. Therefore Taoists conclude that whether we can figure out *Tao* or not always depends upon our own ability to realize it. In other words, the *Tao* is reflected in our minds through the contemplation of Nature. Chapter 17 of *Lao-tzu* shows how the Taoist recognizes nature:

> In highest [antiquity] one did not ever know there were [rulers].
>   Next one loved them and praised them.
>   Next one feared them.
>   Next one despised them.
>   If good faith [of the prince towards the people] is inadequate, good faith [of the people towards the ruler] will be wanting.
>   Thoughtful were [the sage rulers] valuing their words!
>   When the work was done and things went smoothly, the people all said: 'We have done it ourselves!'

As I have already pointed out, an ideal state for Taoists is the one in which a ruler hides his true identity in order to equalize himself with his people, and accordingly no one perceives the benign sway that this virtuous prince holds. Lao-tzu names such a state of ruling 'natural'. Therefore it can be concluded that the ideal society is impossible unless the ruler voluntarily realizes the significance of hiding his identity.

Men and nature

Arnold J. Toynbee, on his visit to Japan in 1967, delivered a lecture in Kyoto, in which he sounded a warning that the traditional notion built upon a man-centred view might bring ruin upon human beings. What he calls 'a man-centred view' indicates a traditional strain of Western thought, whose idea was typically expressed in the well-known words of Prothagoras, 'Man is a measure of all things'. We can possibly come to the extreme view of concluding that men are, arrogantly enough, permitted to ignore the presence of God and to conquer nature freely. The problem Toynbee presented was very serious. We are faced by the dilemma of developing scientific technology or establishing harmony with nature. How can we combine these two ways into a whole? That the Japanese had established an unique culture in harmony with nature was highly appreciated by Toynbee. However, Japanese culture has its origin in ancient China, where profound philosophical views of nature were widespread. Also, wisdom as to how to establish harmony between scientific technologies and nature was already acquired by the ancient Chinese people. Regrettably enough, lack of space prevents us from discussing this point further; nevertheless we can easily find adequate examples in Chinese science, especially in the field of medicine.

As far as our attention centres only upon human society, the realization of ideal equality is hardly possible. Above all, we should devise a means to equalize ourselves with nature. Equality can be achieved, perhaps, not by conquering nature, but by securing harmony with it. Such an idea is easily produced by Taoist philosophy, for, according to it, both men and nature were generated from *tao* and therefore they are in brotherhood.

The maternal principle of Taoist philosophy

As discussed above, Taoist cosmogeny teaches that all things, men as well as the world of nature, sprung forth from *tao* and that they constantly draw their life from it. Therefore, in other words, all existence is no less than manifold manifestations of *tao* itself and accordingly *tao* is the mother of everything. Chapter 25 of *Lao-tzu* says:

> There was something in a state of fusion before heaven and earth were formed. How tranquil, how void it is; it stands alone and changes not, it permeates universally and never tires. It may be regarded as the mother of All–under–heaven.

Also Chapter 52 reads:

> All–under–heaven has a beginning which may be regarded as the mother of All–under–heaven. Having found the mother one may know the children.

If, knowing children, one still keeps to the mother, until the end of his life one is not in peril.

In these passages, the *tao* is likened to a mother, and is often called 'the dark female'. For example, Chapter 6 of *Lao-tzu* states thus:

'The valley spirit never dies'; this refers to the dark female.
'The gate of the dark female'; this refers to the root of heaven and earth.
In fibrous ramifications it is ever present, its acting never ceases.'

'The dark female' and 'the valley spirit' in Taoist terminology indicate a maternal being, that is, the *tao*. Both of these phrases are thus metaphorical, because they suggest a gate through which all things are produced. The metaphor of 'valley' is often used in *Lao-tzu*, for example, in Chapters 6, 15, 28, 39 and 41, and in each case it expresses *tao* symbolically. In other cases, *Lao-tzu* expresses *tao* by using the word 'female'.

In *Lao-tzu* we find that *tao* is likened, without exception, to feminine and maternal beings. Of course, the feminine nature is a metaphor of the matrix from which all existence is produced. In addition, the feminine nature is essentially soft and yielding, and this idea is closely associated with *Lao-tzu*'s expressions. It is well known that Confucianism, another model of Chinese thought, esteems highly the idea of Jen (humanity), the Confucian type of humanism. In general, Confucian ethics are made for a family organization, in which the idea of filial devotions matters most; Confucian philosophy is built upon its paternal principle. Also in Christianity, God himself is often called 'Father'. In contrast, Taoism esteems highly the maternal principle by naming the *tao*, the absolute principle of its philosophy, 'Mother'. Although the Taoist priesthood consists predominantly of male persons, it goes without saying that their philosophy is built upon the *tao*, the maternal principle.

As Chinese history shows us, at the end of the Ching dynasty, in the nineteenth century, the Taiping Rebellion broke out under the leadership of Hung Hsiu-ch'Uan. Astonishingly enough, inside the rebel army, the equal division of land between men and women was already established. It is noteworthy that they identified their idea of 'Taiping' with the ideal society that the ancient Kung-yang scholars had dreamed; they developed the idea of 'Tatung' which was expounded in *Li-chi*, one of the most important Confucian scriptures. The members of the Taiping Rebellion endeavoured to realize their ideal society, in which all the nations were combined into a whole and all men and women would live in an equal and warless state. Their view of human equality, as some scholars pointed out, was influenced greatly by the fundamental idea of Taoist philosophy.

Sun Wen's three principles and Taoism

In this section I would like to discuss the fact that the political thought of Sun Wen (1866–1925), the best known leader of modern China, was influenced by the Taoist view of equality.

When Sun Wen was born, China had seriously suffered under the invasions of the major powers. After the Opium War the powers actively struggled with one another for domination over China. At that time, Sun Wen bravely forced China to turn its face away from the tradition of a despotic monarchy that it had been maintaining for thousands of years; he endeavoured to introduce a democratic spirit into his homeland. He carefully considered the subject of human equality and at last established a system of political thought called San-Min Chu-I, the Three Principles of the People.

His idea of the Three Principles was established under the influence of Henry George. Although Sun Wen had read his *Progress and Poverty* with appreciation during his stay in London, he actively combined the Western idea with Chinese traditional philosophy into a whole. Therefore we should value his original ability to unite these different traditions. He made severe criticisms of Marxism and looked for the way to harmonize the manifold conflicts of social classes. We can conclude that he also belonged to the traditional strain of Chinese philosophy. According to Sun Wen, the spirit of true communism is expressed, not in Marxism, but in the philosophy founded by Lao-tzu and Chuang-tzu.

He also insisted that true universalism could be in no way realized by imperialistic means; instead, we should follow the spirit of Tatung. The idea of Tatung, as mentioned earlier, is written in *Li-chi*, especially in a chapter named 'Liyun'. *Li-chi* describes the ideal society thus: the king's throne is open to common people; each person's position depends upon his ability; persons of both sexes and all ages are equal; all properties and labours are shared uniformly; and therefore every member of society is able to live without any strife. The idea of Tatung was restored by Kang Yu-wei, a philosopher of the nineteenth century, and after that exerted a serious influence upon Chinese revolutionary movements. In Kang Yu-wei's idea of Tatung the traditional Chinese vision of equality is properly embodied, and it is also closely related to Taoist philosophy.

What Sun Wen calls 'San–Min Chu-I' is composed of three principles, nationalism, democracy and socialism.

Sun Wen divides the members of society into three classes, *hsien-chih hsien-chiao*, the class of philosophers, *hou-chih hou-chiao*, the class of bureaucracy, and *pu-chih pu-chiao*, the class of common people. We will see that, historically, the peculiar conditions of China led him to this position.

The Marxist view of equality, generally stated, is founded upon the idea that the wealth of society can be distributed to the proletariat by destroying the members of the privileged minority and bourgeoisie. In contrast, Sun Wen dreams of an ideal society in which all common people ascend the throne, and in so doing wealth is equally shared. His idea is closely associated with Chuang-tzu's. In *Chuang-tzu*, especially in a chapter called '*Chi-wu lun pien*', Chuang-tzu's philosophy is outlined in many contradictory expressions: we can identify T'ai-shan, great mountains, with the smallest thing, or a fur with the biggest thing; we can regard P'eng-tsu, a legendary hero who prolonged his life over eight hundred years, as a poor man who has suffered a premature death, or a child who died young can be seen as one who has enjoyed his long life. When we understand that he speaks in terms of what is called *unio mystica*, 'a mystic identification', these comments will no longer be contradictory. Such an identification can occur only in the mystic state in which, if we use the Upanishad terms, the *ātman* and *Brahmān* are integrated into one. All things which were born from *tao* are also destined to return into *tao* again. Once we have succeeded in lifting ourselves up to a precipitous summit of *unio mystica*, we are, without difficulty, able to observe a whole world reflected in the smallest thing like a fur, or to realize that great mountains are a small thing in comparison with the world itself. For a person who stands on this occult summit and takes his survey, there is no discrimination among 'All–under–heaven': consequently everything is equal to everything else. This idea is emphatically stated in *Chuang-tzu*.

Conception of human nature

Taoism as a philosophy of life

Taoism is a religion greatly concerned with life. Therefore, it aims at obtaining longevity and immortality. In Taoist terms, life is composed of *ch'i* (*pneuma*), and in order to make one's spirit imperishable, first of

all, the body which is the receptacle of the spirit must be immortal-
ized. To secure such immortality, it becomes necessary to prepare
medicines and practice breathing exercises, gymnastics (*tao-yin*), and
sexual hygiene (*fang-chung-shu*). Of the medicines, there were elixirs,
tonics and pills for medical treatment. Alchemy, the chief aim of
which was to discover how to change oridinary metals into gold and
silver, herbology and the Chinese school of medicine known as *kampō*
developed in connection with Taoism. Taoism as a religion contains a
scientific aspect and recognizes the value of technical skill.

Further, to make one's spirit imperishable, believers practiced
ch'ingssu and *shou-i*, the Taoist methods of meditation by which one
unites oneself with *tao*, which is the all-embracing first principle
through which the universe has come into being. This is closely
associated with mysticism. And it was the philosophy of Lao-tzu and
Chuang-tzu which gave Taoist mysticism its philosophical structure.
The Lao-Chuang philosophy brought about a world of inner transcendence, a surrealist world, as it were, by negating the practical
world through Taoist practices. Taoism respects life, so it naturally
approves of human desire, the source of life. To immortalize life
means to make desire something eternal. To realize this, spiritualization is necessary, and the Lao–Chuang philosophy was successful in
spiritualizing desire through its negative Taoist practices. This shows
that Taoism has in itself a strong subjective consciousness and self-
restraint.

The Taoism thus described above was solely for the intellectuals,
and at the base of this there was religious Taoism for the masses.
Religious or popular Taoism pursued desires with which men were
born in an attempt to establish various methods for satisfaction in this
world. Popular Taoism at first was closely related to the cult of
shen-hsien (spirit and immortality) worship, but finally became a
worldly religion whose exclusive aim was obtaining happiness, wealth
and longevity. Compared with philosophical Taoism, it lacks intellectual flavour and a sense of independence as a religion. However, it is
distinct from other popular beliefs quite dependent upon help from
without in that it emphasizes its ethical character.

The thought that affirms desire in 'Pao-p'u-tzu'

In the opening part (*Nei-p'ien*), 'Ch'ang-hsuan-p'ien' of his work
Pao-p'u-tzu (*ca* AD 317), Ko Hung, who represents the Taoist thinkers

in the Six Dynasties Period, writes about *hsüan*, the supreme first principle of the universe as follows:

> *Hsüan* is the origin of nature and permeates the myriad species of creation. It is called *wei* (subtle), because it is dark and deep. It is also called *miao* as it moves endlessly over a vast course. It goes up high, covering the sky and extends in all directions. It shines brighter than the sun and the moon, and moves quicker than lightning. It travels like lightning and shoots like a star. It is like deep, clear water, and yet it breaks into floating clouds. Permeating all things, it becomes *yu* (being), but being identified with *chi*, it becomes *wu* (non-being). It sinks into the earth and yet rises up to the sky to float above the stars. Its strength defies comparison with any metal of stone and yet it is softer than dew. Although it is square, it cannot be measured. It is circular, but a compass cannot measure it. Coming but unseen, going but unpursued, it causes Heaven and Earth to be as they are. It makes rain and the clouds. Filling Heaven, it moulds the *Yin-yang* principles of the universe, breathes out the beginning of the world and melts myriad things. Scattering twenty-eight mansions (*hsü*), it creates the universe, presides over nature, and breathes the four seasons. It creates dead silence, sending forth pleasing fragrance. Preventing drought, increasing cleanliness, it thus controls the Yellow River and the Wei River. It swells but never overflows. One cannot drain it out. One cannot add nor take from it. Therefore, where there is *hsüan*, there is endless happiness. When *hsüan* disappears, one's body feels exhausted and one's spirit dies.

This explains the experience of mysticism in which one gains union with the ultimate power which creates the myriad things in the universe and the origin of endless life. The concept of *tao* in the Lao–Chuang philosophy is expressed as *hsüan*, which indicates more religious and mystical functions. As seen above, one who is one with *hsüan* is able to enjoy happiness endlessly.

The above-quoted passages describe the magical power of running freely in the sky as a function of *hsüan*. This is not mere imagination, but the substance of a mystical experience. Taoists' descriptions of *shen-jen* (spiritual men) and *t'ien-hsien* (celestial immortals) are based on this experience. Although *t'ien-hsien* are described in detail in the *Pao-p'u-tzu*, here in this chapter I would like to take up *ti-hsien* (terrestrial immortals). According to the 'Tui-su-p'ien' of the *Pao-p'u-tzu*, P'eng-tsu, the Chinese Methuselah, speaks as follows:

> In Heaven, there are many celestial officials and great gods, while new immortals who are under them in rank have to undergo hardship and work hard like servants. So, one need not take the trouble to go to Heaven. There were once persons who attained the state of *hsien* and flew far into the sky with wings which grew on their bodies, but this magical power led them to

transgress the way of men. According to Taoist magic, as a sparrow assumes the shape of a clam and a pheasant transforms itself into a big clam, so the human body can assume any shape. This, however, is also contrary to the way of men. The way of men is to eat delicious food, wear light, warm clothes, enjoy sex, be intelligent enough to enter civil service, have strong bones and a good complexion, never lose one's vigor even when one grows old, prolong life to be able to work as an official or stay home at will, never let cold, heat, wind, or dampness injure one's health, guard against demons and spirits, protect oneself from armed struggles and various poisons, never worry about sorrow or joy, and care for neither praise nor blame. This is the attitude which should be valued. One who leads a life of a hermit in a mountain, discarding his wife and children, will never be respected by others, if he cuts himself off from the ties of human nature and has no more feeling than a stone.

With the desire to live, various kinds of spiritual or materialistic desires swell up. Development of these desires in the same dimension, however, will eventually lead to what Thomas Hobbes called '*Bellum omnium contra omnes*'. In an attempt to forestall such a possible situation, Taoism conceived of the purification of desire. More concretely, this constitutes an attempt to unite oneself with *hsüan*, with the ultimate source of life in the universe. In order to realize this, it was necessary to negate one's worldly desires through various practices.

Next, let us consider the problem of science and intelligence in Taoism. When mysticism is combined with pantheistic thought, one is led to experience oneself as united with the origin of the universe and able to manipulate the secrets of the universe. As is stated in the *Pao-p'u-tzu*, man, the lord of all creation, is so intelligent that he may use all things in the universe and study the principles of nature by pursuit of learning. Furthermore, by applying the result thereof to the making of medicine, longevity can be obtained.

The thought that affirms desire in the Lao–Chuang philosophy

I think that the ideological base of Taoism lies in the Lao–Chuang philosophy. It is generally accepted that Lao–Chuang thought advocates asceticism, but I do not agree with this view. In my opinion, what actually constitutes *wu-yü*, non-desire, as one of the philosophical concepts of Lao–Chuang, is the purification of desire, not its prohibition.

What forms the basis of Lao–Chuang thought is the idea of softness and weakness (*jou-jo*). Lao-tzu explains why the Tao is soft and weak by likening it to water. In Chapter 8 of Lao-tzu's *Tao-te-ching* the following passage is found: 'The highest goodness is like water. The goodness of water consists in benefiting the ten thousand things without ever striving. It stays in the lowest place which all men loathe. Therefore, it comes near to the Way' (Duyvendak translation p. 34). Another statement on water is made in Chapter 78: 'There is in all the world nothing that is softer or weaker than water, but in attacking what is hard and strong, nothing surpasses it' (ibid. p. 101).

Water that is soft and weak is the spring of life and often demonstrates that it has the strongest power in the world. In China, where irrigation and flood control of the Yellow River is said to have developed the country, this fact was a truth which the Chinese people could readily understand.

Tao as conceived by Lao-tzu was pantheistic. His cosmology is well reflected in the following passage: 'The Way produced one; one produced two; two produced three; three produced ten thousand things' (*ibid*. p. 42). That the Way (*tao*) was understood in a pantheistic sense can also be seen in the 'Chih-pei-yu p'ien' of the *Chuang-tzu*. Asked where the so-called Tao is, Chuang-tzu answers: 'There is no place where it does not exist . . . It is in an ant . . . It is in the panic grass . . . It is in earthenware tiles . . . It even is in excrement.'

Tao is the source of life in the universe and exists within all the myriad things. To unify oneself mystically with the Tao thus means the affirmation of desire of all living things as well as the encouragement of their creation. But one should not forget that before unifying with the Tao, one must experience self-forgetfulness as non-desire. Yet non-desire does not mean asceticism. It means spiritualization of desire by means of which unbound desire can be liberated. This also implies the negation of worldly desire through practices such as deeds of self-forgetfulness done in the world of contradictions and confrontation.

There is an episode about P'ao Ting, a butcher who cuts up oxen with his knife, in the 'Yang-sheng-shu p'ien' of the *Chuang-tzu*. The edge of this knife never breaks, even after the cutting of thousands of oxen. Following the physiological structure of the oxen's bodies, the knife enters easily into joints and crevices, which a less skilled person would miss easily. P'ao Ting's way of moving the knife is led by spirit-like wisdom. He never sees it with the naked eye. Senses stop working, while spiritualized desire (*shen-yü*) is at work. It is called mastering the knife (*yu-jen*) because the movement is executed so skilfully. Such a state of mind is attained by self-forgetfulness, which in turn is acquired through a practical negation of the existing world. Through this practical negation, *shen-yü*, that is, endless perfection and spiritualization of desire, can be attained.

It was Kuo Hsiang (d. AD 312) of the Six Dynasties Period who reorganized Lao–Chuang's method of negating the existing world through practices into the theory of non–being (*wu*). Lao-tzu's negative approach to the existing world by various practices had its origin in his passive way of living in politically unstable times. In the case of Chuang-tzu, his attitude towards life became more introspective. Such an attitude led him to adopt the principle of complying with his own self and living free from worldly cares. In the Six Dynasties Period, Kuo Hsiang established the theory of how to attain the world of inner transcendence, sublimating his inner self and the outer world. Kuo Hsiang expounds a method to conquer afflictions (*shang*). (See his commentary on the 'Hsiao–yao–yu p'ien' of the *Chuang-tzu*.)

According to Kuo Hsiang's method, primary importance is given to the concept of not avoiding afflictions or trying to overcome them, but rather adjusting oneself to them intently. By doing so one is able to unify oneself with the very afflictions one encounters, to even attain a stage where one is content with them, thereby overcoming all afflictions completely. It seems to me that this concept of Kuo Hsiang's is somewhat akin to the philosophy of existentialism in our time, though as a characteristic of Lao–Chuang philosophy, the former puts much more emphasis on human desire than the latter. In his commentary to the *Chuang-tzu*, Kuo Hsiang states that everything produces itself and does not issue from anything else, using terms like *tzu-wu* or *tzu-ts'ao*. He also says: 'If one penetrates the nature of all things and understands it perfectly, then there will be nothing one cannot unify oneself with . . . We call this the nature of things (*hsing*), because it is fully spontaneous.' In Kuo Hsiang's philosophy, nature (*tzu-jan*) is a stage in which the unification of oneself and others is attained — a surrealistic world based on the Tao. It is the concept of nature which pays respect to human activity. In this philosophy, we can find the oneness of 'fate' and 'freedom'. Upon such a self which defies any standardization, spiritualization of desire can be achieved.

The world in which desire is spiritualized is inevitably surrealistic. The story of the mythical great *p'eng* bird who ascends on a whirlwind to a height of ninety thousand *li* in the first chapter of the *Chuang-tzu* illustrates the surrealistic world. Lao-tzu's *Tao-te-ching* explains in its first chapter the relationship between the Tao and all things of the universe by employing such terms as 'invariable names', 'variable names', 'invariable non-being', 'invariable being'. In the invariable non-being, Lao-tzu sees the functioning (the secret essence) of the Tao, while in the invariable being, he wishes to see the borders (*chiao*) of all things. These two, namely, the secret essence of Tao and the borders of all things, correspond, but are different in name. So, we may say they are two but one and yet they are one but two. In short, the Tao and all things in the universe are a unified one. Such a mystic character of Tao Lao-tzu calls the Mystery of Mysteries or the Gate of Wonders. It is the world of this inner transcendence that I call the surrealistic world.

The 'Ch'i-wu-lun' chapter of the *Chuang-tzu* relates a story about Chuang-tzu's dream in which he became a butterfly. He was fluttering here and there joyously, forgetting that the butterfly was none other than himself. Suddenly he awoke to find that it was a dream. Yet to Chuang-tzu, it seemed uncertain whether he became a butterfly in his dream or a butterfly became Chuang-tzu himself in the dream. Common sense tells us that there is a distinction between dream and reality. But who guarantees that the dream Chuang-tzu dreamed was not the reality and that the reality that surrounded him was not a dream? This stage of *wu-hua* through which everything changes freely and endlessly is based on reality and yet transcends reality. This is what I refer to as surrealistic. It is in this surrealistic world that the spiritualization of desire can be attained.

Conclusion

1. On the waves of modernization, equality is largely established from the outside. Though this is certainly a necessity, for the achievement of true equality an interior self-realization is basically very important. In Asia one can find a long tradition of philosophy as well as religion being concerned with veritable interior equality. The equality meant here is the foundation for the freedom of man's liberated personality. Taoist humanism postulates the purification of desire. This purification or spiritualization of desire is a negative affirmation of desire. Once purified, desire turns into the true self of the deeper layers of one's mind and heart, it is thus productive in the fields of art and culture. This means unlimited joy and happiness; it is the outset of the realm of surrealism. The real equality is to be built on this purification of desire.

2. A man is often discouraged in his life and through this painful experience he keenly sympathizes with other's sufferings. Such a state of discouraged mind is named by Jaspers '*Scheitern*', and also called by Kuo Hsiang '*shang*', that is, 'afflictions', and the state of being 'forlorn' in *Lao-tzu*. This is the source of religious awareness, that is to say, a man is enforced to face an absolute being by his discouraged experience. Let us recall the famous passage of Matthew 5: 'Blessed are the poor in spirit, for theirs is the kingdom of heaven.'

3. In Taoism, the philosophy of weakness and softness, explained as the ethics of water, plays a central part. Water is weak and soft on the one hand, yet it is also the essence of all life, and on the other hand, it has a marvellous aggressive power, exemplified in floods. The Tao, which is the source of all life in the universe, is symbolized by water. If everybody possessed the life-force and the fighting power of water, then everyone, though he be weak and humble, would be able to overcome the strong and powerful. Moreover, in the government by philosophers proposed by Taoism the ruler is supposed to descend all the way down to the lower strata of society like water and perform a policy entirely shaped by non-action and nature. This way the equality of society as a whole is established, the peace of the world secured.

4. In contrast with Confucianism, which has developed the idea of patriarchy and men's predominance over women, Taoism has paid special attention to feminine nature and set forth the doctrine of 'softness and weakness'. Although the Taoist priests were, like those of other religions, dominated by males, the priesthood itself was not always prohibited for women. For example, the founder of Mao-shan p'ai or Shang ch'ing p'ai, one of the most influential sects of Taoism, was Wei fu-jen or Wei hua-ts'un, who was Wei-shu's daughter. And also it is well known that Hsi-wang-mu (the Queen of the West) is one of the most reverend deities in the Taoist pantheon.

5. According to the Taoist philosophy, all things in the universe are equally precious because Tao produces all of them, that is to say, they are all manifestations of Tao. The Taoist concept is reflected in Sun Wen's words: 'all common people ascend the throne and in so doing the wealth and power are equally shared'. Truth is open to every individual, though few are aware of it. Such a Taoist situation has a strange resemblance to the society of modern ages;

a group of scientists, who are in a small minority in our society, takes the initiative in society's development, whereas the multitude is ignorant of scientific technology. Although, in modern democratic society, people are likely to claim their rights, they have forgotten high ideals and they are compelled to make themselves 'smaller'. We have to restore belief in internal absolute values which are deeply buried in religious and cultural traditions.

6. Sun Wen's classification of society into three classes has nothing to do with Indian castes. In Chinese history, even at the period of feudalism, partial changes of social classification often occurred and sometimes emperors and high officials rose from the lower class. For example, Liu Pang (247–195 BC), the founder of Han Dynasty, was of low birth, and Chu Yuan-chang (1323–98), the first emperor of the Ming Dynasty, was a son of the soil.

7. In contrast with Confucianism, which is the ideology for a ruling class, Taoism always stands on the side of the poor and non-official intellectuals. In China, poor peasants sometimes rose in rebellion against rulers, and, generally speaking, the rebels had firm faith in Taoism.

8. Historical consciouness and technological reformation are two conditions necessary for the egalitarian movement. In old times, these conditions were under the control of religious sects. It goes without saying that Taoism performed an important role in the egalitarian movement of China. In modern ages technological progress leaves religions behind and we are seldom conscious of history. We have to recover those two conditions once again.

9. The humanity of Taoism values man's intelligence especially highly. By means of a mystical union with the Tao, man is assured of not living in strain with the laws of the universe, but rather in accordance with them. Human technical progress when setting out from such a basis will not destroy nature, but provide for man's harmonious living together with nature. In this very harmony man's highest dignity can be found. It is considerably different from the view that man is the centre of the universe which sprang originally from Protagoras.

10. Taoists have paid attention to the variety in nature. They know that nature is divided into abundant and various components and they change and develop in perpetual movement. In the Taoist context the variety of nature has nothing to do with the concept of classification or discrimination. Equality in Taoism does not only

aim at a position where all members within human society are equal, but also proposes harmonious living together of man and nature. This is, in particular, because both man and nature are seen as parts of the Tao.

7 Jewish Perspectives on Equality

Nathan Katz

I should preface my remarks by saying that I will emphaize the *distinctive* contributions of Jewish thought on this question. Being of the Abrahamic family of religions, Judaism shares much in its view with Christianity and Islam. However, there are distinctive points, and my emphasis will be on the uniqueness of the perspectives of the Jewish tradition.

To begin, I should point out two dimensions — or two perspectives — on equality from the Jewish tradition. I would call these the metaphysical dimension, on the one hand, and the messianic dimension on the other.

I will illustrate this metaphysical perspective with reference to a creation symbology devised by Rabbi Isaac Luria. This is not the commonly known creation mythology found in Genesis, but a very tantalizing and influential metaphor taken from the Kabbalah. According to Rabbi Luria, prior to creation all that existed was the *ayn soph*. *Ayn* is the Hebrew word for 'not', and *soph* means a cognitive limit or 'bottom'. So, primordially there is this fathomless reality, an undifferentiated fathomlessness. In order to make room for a world, this fathomless reality contracted itself, limited itself by the process of *tzimtzum*. It is then and only then that we can begin to use the terms 'G–d' in the conventional sense. Creation is the ongoing process made possible by this splitting of the *ayn soph* into two principles of divinity: YHVH and the *Shekhinah*. To G–d, or YHVH as He is known in our Scriptures, we can ascribe such characteristics as maleness, concern for history, dwelling in the sky, and so forth.

Simultaneously there emerges His counterpart, the *Shekhinah*, which is the indwelling presence, the immanent, female, earth-orientated, non-historical aspect of divinity. Originally, then, there is an androgyny which knows no distinctions (and I can think of no more egalitarian notion than that) which, in order for there to be creation, splits itself, divides itself into halves, into male and female principles. (This mythology is remarkably similar, by the way, to one found in the *Chāndogya Upaniṣad* of Hinduism, in which the One, having divided itself as sport, seeks to regain its primordial unity through the other, which is not other than the One.) This female principle, the *Shekhinah*, the indwelling, is immanent in all of creation, perhaps most significantly in all humans as what we call *ruach*, the animating principle, the breath of G–d, the soul. Here we find something shared with all Western or Semitic religions, the idea of an indwelling divinity, a spark as we call it (*nitzotzsh*) in all people, which has absolute sanctity and intrinsic value.

To sum up, then, we find in Jewish literature the idea of a metaphysical, primordial unity, immanent in all humans, as a basis for equality. As we find this egalitarian unity prior to creation (and throughout history *in potentia*), we also find an analogous egalitarian notion inhabiting Jewish thinking about the end of creation.

Here I am referring to Jewish messianic thinking. At the end of time, according to G–d's plan, an egalitarian unity is established through the divine agency of the messiah or *mosheach*. Jewish messianic thought directly addresses those three areas of strife and inequality which dominate history: race, class, and gender.

Regarding the concept of race (and of course the term 'race' does not appear in the Hebrew Bible; the term used is 'nation' or *goy*), we find in our daily liturgy the following prayer: 'At that (messianic) time, nations shall no longer take up weapons against other nations; swords shall be beaten into farming implements.' Here we find as essential to the messianic promise the idea that there will be peace, respect, and amity among nations. As for issues of class, we also find in our liturgy: 'Every man beneath his vine and fig tree shall live in peace and unafraid.' I know this might sound very modernistic, but to me this verse is speaking of the relationship of people to the means of production. That is, if each person has their own vine and fig tree, their own means of production, then the distinction of owner and worker, a basis of enmity and strife, will dissolve.

The messianic promise also addresses issues of sexism. Rabbi Luria's mythology, mentioned before, promises that the estranged male and female principles, which throughout history long for each other as do lovers in separation, finally reunite. The enmity between the sexes embedded in the Eden mythology finally becomes harmony.

So it seems that the three historic foci of strife — classism, racism, and sexism — are resolved in the messianic age. It is this promise of such an age that makes our current, alienated history sensible, as a condition which is not final. The promise also guides our actions and attitudes through pre-messianic history. All of this is fairly straightforward: that once upon a time there was harmony which somehow became out of joint as the condition for there being a world, and that this harmony or *shalom* will come again at the end of time. With this much as background, I can now indicate what is really distinctive about Jewish thought: the status of the time in between the primordial and the messianic, what we call exile or *galut*. To appreciate some of the nuances of Jewish exilic thinking, I want to just mention three basic categories or structures of Jewish thought: the rabbinic approach, the prophetic standpoint, and finally exilic theology.

In the rabbinic tradition, we are guided by the maxim taught by one of our great saints: the way to G–d is through man. Despite its male voice, the idea is that we have access to the divine only through each other. It seems that a religious tradition has essentially two options regarding the nature and status of the person. Either one accepts an isolated, individualistic conception, or one holds to a communalistic or network notion of the person. I don't see how it is really possible for a religion finely to balance between both; somehow a choice is made and, given such a choice, Judaism would certainly opt for the latter framework. This communal view of the person is accepted by all truly ancient religions, and one finds very similar conceptions in Hinduism and Confucianism as well.

Given this framework, our rabbis displayed some surprisingly humanistic approaches in their interpretations of the Law. The Law is a system of injunctions, prescriptions, and proscriptions covering all aspects of human life — from what we eat, to what we wear, to what we do when we first awaken in the morning, to what we say, and so forth (not unlike ritualistic Hinduism). The rabbis distinguished two types of sin. One is the sin against G–d, and the other is the sin against other people. It is very wisely said that G–d can forgive only sins against G–d, but G–d cannot forgive sins against other people. This can be done only by the offended party.

For example, consider our observances surrounding the holiest day of our calendar, Yom Kippur, the Day of Atonement. Yom Kippur is preceded by ten days of repentance, when it is incumbent upon every Jew to reflect upon the past year, to see whether there have been any transgressions against G–d or against other people. These ten days are a time set aside for rectifying these transgressions. Before one may participate in the ritual observance of Yom Kippur, one must have made amends for these transgressions directly to the party involved. This reflects the humanistic emphasis of our rabbis, who always maintained that any law of the Torah could be abrogated under certain circumstances — if a life is in danger, for example. Thus, the sanctity of human life has a priority over the divinity of the Law, should the two principles conflict.

Similarly, we have two kinds of procession in the Jewish tradition: one for marriage and one for funerals. So the rabbis asked: which, according to our Law, has the right of way, the marriage procession or the funeral procession, should they meet at a crossroad? The answer, of course, is that the funeral procession must give way to the marriage procession because it is life, after all, that is the consummate value, life and dignity.

There is one other point in the rabbinic tradition which I find most intriguing in the context of our discussion, and this is the notion of Jubilee. You may know that in our calendar every seventh day is called a *shabat* or sabbath, which is a day when we refrain from work, when we reflect, meditate, evaluate the week. Similarly, every seventh year is a sabbatical year, when academics have some leisure to think and read, when our fields lie fallow. Expanding the range of this cycle, every fiftieth year (that is, seven times seven plus one) is what we call a Jubilee, which I take to be a radically egalitarian idea. According to the Torah, the Jubilee is a time when all wealth in a society is equally distributed among all people. There is a profound insight here: that it is not enough for there to be a revolution leading to the equitable distribution of wealth once and for all. The Torah seems to anticipate much contemporary human experience in foreseeing that such a once-and-for-all redistribution of wealth will eventually ossify into the formation of new classes and privileges, that hierarchy will reimpose itself despite our most egalitarian and humanistic motives. So every fifty years, roughly one in a lifetime, a total redistribution of all the resources of a society is recommended. These are a few of the humane, egalitarian teachings of our rabbis.

Our prophets, of course, are well known for their passionate commitments to social justice. I think it is fair to say that the Hebrew prophets were the first people to come up with the idea that kingship or political power is a human institution, and therefore subject to human criticism. The notion of divine kingship, for example that the Pharaoh of Egypt is G–d Himself, is explicitly rejected.

Like many other ancient religions, our sacred text contains a narrative story, the history of our people. One of the most important events in this history, perhaps the paradigmatic event in the entire narrative line, is the story of the Exodus. You may know the story: once upon a time the Jewish people were held as slaves in Egypt, and then somehow or other they managed to be liberated from slavery, wandered in the desert, received the revelation of Torah at Sinai, and eventually entered the promised land of Israel. Jewish thinking about this and other paradigmatic events follows a *midrashic* framework. The story is the given of the tradition; it is unarguable, non-propositional. Given the story, then, the question becomes how we interpret it. The distinctive contribution of Jewish thought to such hermeneutical questions is that one never leaves the particulars of the story, but by analogy applies the story to other cases. Just this hermeneutical method was applied by Freud to the neurotic's dreams and actions, but that is another tale to tell. This is the essence of the *midrashic* approach: the concreteness of events must never be lost, but the significance of the events is not limited to their concreteness. We were slaves to the Pharaoh in Egypt, and G–d with an outstretched arm led us out of bondage in Egypt to freedom, self-determination, and dignity in Israel. Then, by analogy, we reason and see that according to the divine imperative, all peoples should enjoy the same freedom, self-determination, and dignity as we did: such is G–d's will. History becomes the medium through which we know G–d, history as the narrative story. It is through attention to our history that, for us, we are able to make more general, ethical statements about history as a whole. We never leave the concreteness of events. This is a crucial point, because history — which is the narrative between the primordial oneness and the final, messianic events — all such history is the history of particulars. Right now we have no universals; all we have are the particulars from which we may analogically reason. It is the human condition, at least until the messianic dawning, that we are separate individuals and separate peoples. This philosophy of particulars means that these differences among us are not a problem so much as a delight; that if G–d had wanted us to have one religion He would have given us one (although some people think that he has already done just that).

This particularistic view of history is a radically anti-hegemonistic viewpoint. There is no one ideology, no one religion, no one language, which we should all speak, believe, or act upon. Were we to think otherwise, then it would be as though believing we should have but one letter, A, rather than a whole alphabet. The world, I feel, would be profoundly diminished by that. This world, which seems at times a cacophony of diverse cultures and quarrels, really in some divine sense is a delight, a luxury, a larger harmony, and most of all a terrible challenge. Our particularistic view entails that we define ourselves and that every people should define themselves, that there should be no hegemonistic imposition or definition, that semantic power should not rest with an elite possessing transcultural 'truth', but that semantic power should be democratized. This process of self-definition is encapsulated in our much maligned and much misunderstood claim to chosenness.

The doctrine of chosenness often raises very touchy issues, and it somewhat resembles the national charter myth of the Sinhalese people as contained in the *Mahāvaṁsa*. It raises problems, but it also has tremendous positive potentiality. We feel ourselves to have been singled out by G–d for a certain mission in the world. We feel ourselves to be unique. What I am asking you to see is that, conceptually, uniqueness is not a comparative category. One thing cannot be 'more or less unique' than another. Given the view of the radical particularity of history, the only position we can take is that all phenomena, all particulars, are unique. So, when we claim ourselves to be chosen, we make no statement whatsoever about other peoples and the ways in which they arrive at self-definition and self-determination. They may well be chosen also, but that is for them to say, not for us.

Many peoples in history have borrowed from and adapted our mythologies to suit their conditions. One such people are the Christians; another are the Rastafarians of Jamaica. This is rather flattering from a Jewish perspective; it is a wonderful thing that our history is significant for others. We have no quarrel with such claims, so long as we are all allowed to rest in our uniqueness, our particularity, our chosenness. Where we might have to take issue is when some people claim that their chosenness somehow displaces ours. This would be a stubborn understanding of the chosenness idea, one which does not evidence sufficient appreciation for the particularity of history which is the post-primordial and pre-messianic human condition. Quite the contrary, what we are chosen to do is to delight in, to revel in, to affirm wholeheartedly the uniqueness and particularlity of each nation so that other nations, too, might discover the ways in which they themselves are chosen. This is the sense I make out of the Prophet Isaiah's idea that we should be a nation of priests. He teaches that we should show by example our way of understanding our own history as divinely inspired and, by implication, how every people can understand their own history as also divinely sanctioned. This divine sanction of each nation's history means that all national identities must be subordinated to spiritual purposes and identities.

I am very well aware of the danger of certain appropriations of this mythological structure, but I think it could be seen as similar to the Sinhalese sense of their own national calling to be subservient to the *dharma*, as embodied in the *dharmadvīpa* ideal. The mythology of the Buddha's visits to Sri Lanka means that the *dharma* is the *raison d'être* for the Sinhalese nation. *Sinhaladvīpa*, or nationalism in the ordinary sense, must be transformed into *dharmadvīpa*. If this rationale becomes reversed, then it becomes a dangerous and potentially chauvinistic idea. There is a similar principle operative here: that the nation becomes subservient to and dependent upon a principle, and that true national identity in its particularity embodies that which is closest to a universal which we have in our world.

This brings us directly to the notion of exile, which has been a dominant theme in Jewish thinking since the time of Isaiah. Indeed, entire theologies of exile have emerged from the Jewish people which evidence a profound creativity and mark an utterly distinctive contribution to human thought.

If the Exodus from Egypt and the liberation of the Jewish people from slavery is *religiously* significant, if it reflects a divine imperative, then so too do the tragic events in Jewish history. The paradigm of tragedy in Jewish history (before the Holocaust) is when our homeland, Israel, was lost and when we were taken from our land into exile in Babylonia. The powerful, tragic story of such estrangement compels other peoples to understand their history in terms of our mythic structures. Bob Marley adapts the Prophet Isaiah's words when he sings:

> By the rivers of Babylon, where we lay down,
> Oh, how we wept when we remembered Zion . . .

We find ourselves in Babylonia, humiliated, defeated, suffering, and again enslaved, tantalized by the memory of freedom. I cannot keep tears from my eyes when I listen to Marley's beautiful borrowing from our story. There are indeed times in life, on both individual and national levels, when we experience this sort of humiliation. We suffer and we may have no choice but to suffer. But the point is not to try and escape suffering, but how to make suffering sufferable, how to find a divine meaning even in humiliation:

> How can we sing our Lord's song in a strange land?

In Isaiah's categories, this means that the Jewish people must now become 'a nation among nations', *yet* 'a light unto nations', even 'a nation of priests'. For him, to bear witness to G–d's sovereignty over history, especially under such tragic circumstances, becomes suffering's 'meaning'.

Later Jewish thinkers, reflecting upon exile, spoke of it not only as something particular to the Jewish people, but also as the human condition between creation and redemption. What we say is that history *is* exile, a basic structure adopted *in toto* by Karl Marx. Marx says that, between the paradisal stage of primitive communism and the consummation of history in the withering away of the state, we see history unfolding through struggle, pain, agony and alienation. Of course, Marx would not call this structure of history a *divine* plan, but rather a dynamic inherent in the dialectics of history.

Returning to more orthodox Jewish thought, we find that during the pre-Creation, primordial time, and also during the messianic era, perhaps one could speak coherently about a human essence, a soul or some such notion which makes us equal in G–d's sight, an ultimate egalitarianism if you will. However, in the exile which we inhabit, it makes more sense to talk about a human *condition* than any metaphysical *essence*. Essences are deferred to messianic times; now we may address conditions. Having made this conceptual shift from essence to condition, I think we become open to very humanistic and even proto-existentialist views of human life. It is the condition of exile which we share, a condition we share even with G–d, and there ensues a very complex relationship between the messianic age, which is the promise of addressing all forms of human oppression, and the condition of exile. The messianic promise is one of *différence* in the Derridian, double sense. It is *différence* because it differs from our exilic condition and because it *defers* all ultimates which constitute that promise. To put this point differently, this exilic history makes no sense without the messianic promise, so there emerges this ever-receding promise which is our only source of meaning in this exiled life. Authentic Jewish life means balancing between the promise of redemption and the actuality of exile.

On the notion of redemption, I must hastily indicate a wide divergence between Jewish thinking and that found in other Semitic traditions. For Jews, 'to redeem' is a transitive verb which usually takes 'the world' as its object. There is no notion whatsoever of individual salvation in Judaism. We are taught that the highest good is the redemption of the world. It is no spiritualized world which is redeemed, but *this* world. In Weberian categories, which I generally dislike, Judaism becomes emphatically a 'this-wordly' religion. What the whole purpose of creation entails is the transformation of the 'is' of this world into the 'ought' of redemption.

Again to distinguish: it is well known that Jews believe the messiah is yet to come, and this has become historically a very important teaching. There is no triumphalism. There is a promise, but there is as yet no 'good news'. Why is this point important? Because historically we have seen that those ideologies which proclaim, in one way or another, that the messiah has already come lose the ability and tools for rigorous self-criticism. Prophetic criticism is dialectical in the sense that it seeks to admonish, to change empirical conditions. It remains dialectically connected with that which it criticizes, eschewing that sort of dualistic criticism which dissociates itself from the criticized, as Professor Ruether has ably demonstrated. It is this dialectical character of prophetic criticism that gets lost in proclaiming a triumphalist state of affairs. For example (and these are meant as friendly criticisms for my Marxist and Christian brothers and sisters), if the Marxist believes that the revolution has already come and that the classless society has been established, then who could be criticized for persisting social inequalities? If all evil stems from property and if property has been abolished, then present evils must be ignored or rationalized away. Very similarly, many Christians read into the purported messiahship of Jesus the fact that believers have already been saved, that this world is redeemed. I know there are justifications, but the problem of evil is again left unsolved and either rationalized or spiritualized. If the Church is the triumphant vehicle of the messiahship, then one must look elsewhere to account for the persistence of evil. This 'looking elsewhere' is scapegoating, and this is precisely what one has found repeatedly associated with the history of Christendom. Only a pre-messianic view of history is compatible with both the fact of the persistence of evil and with the prophetic, dialectical criticism which is essential for any progressive world orientation, for the enhancement of egalitarian values.

In conclusion, then, I believe an exilic view of history, the appreciation of the tragic sense of human life, coupled with the messianic promise, allows for the sort of self-criticism necessary to move us towards the promise without pre-empting the divine author of that promise. Emphasizing the incompleteness of human life, and balancing between creation and redemption, are distinctively Jewish bases for our comparative discussion of the meaning of equality.

8   The Concept of Equality in Islamic Thought

Chandra Muzaffar

Equality as an idea is deeply embedded in Islamic philosophy. Its sociological manifestations are also lucidly expressed in both the Quran and the Sunnah (the way of the Prophet Muhammad) on the one hand, and in other Islamic traditions, on the other.

The philosophical basis

To start with, the idea receives support from the philosophical view of what the religion is all about. It is said that Islam is the 'natural religion' of man.[1] By this is meant that it is the way of life, the code of conduct that is most harmonious with the development of man's humanity. And man's humanity is intrinsic to his nature. The right social conditions must be created to enable man's nature — in the sense in which it is used here — to blossom.

By linking Islam to man's nature, the commonality of all human beings is unequivocally established. All human beings are essentially the same — as far as their basic nature goes. It is this that makes them equal.

As an aside, it is this view of Islam as a path that cultivates man's humanity in line with his nature that defies its classification as a religion in the coventional way in which the term is used in Western anthropology. Islam, in other words, is a way of life with values and principles which guide almost every sphere of human existence. The aim of this guidance is to facilitate man's service to God.

The oneness of man which this idea engenders is further reinforced by the Islamic conception of Adam. Adam is the symbol of man — of all human beings. He represents a vital point in the creative evolution of life.[2] He symbolizes the beginning of consciousness — man's consciousness of his own nature and its inclination towards goodness. It is this consciousness which helps to emphasise man's common humanity. Once again, it makes all human beings equal in their awareness of their nature.

However, Adam represents equality in a much more tangible manner. Since all human beings are descended from Adam and Eve, the original pair, they are all equal in their common origin. The Quran repeatedly stresses that this common origin is the basis of human solidarity, of man's equality. More important, since Adam is made from dust, his descendants should remain ever conscious of their humble genesis. Indeed, the Quran reminds man of this as a way of making him perpetually aware of the need to struggle against unjustified inequities and to strive for legitimate equality.

The equality that is related to the position of Adam is developed more thoroughly in the Qurannic concept of Prophecy. The Quran recognizes all the prophets — those it mentions and those it does not mention — who were sent to various lands as legitimate messengers of the same God. It implores humankind not to distinguish one from the other. This implies the universality of truth, on the one hand, and its particular manifestations, on the other. Its relevance to equality lies in two related spheres: first, it shows that the eternal truth, whatever its form or its channel, has the same value, and second, it indicates that the truth is accessible to everyone.

Within the Quran itself there are a number of verses which incorporate these ideas of equality. At one place, for instance, it says: 'Mankind was one single nation, And Allah sent Messengers With Glad tidings and warnings. . . .'[3] At another point it says,

> O mankind: We created You from a single [pair] Of a male and a female And made you into Nations and tribes, that Ye may know each other (Not that ye may despise Each Other). Verily the most honoured of you In the sight of Allah Is [he who is] the most Righteous of you: And Allah has full knowledge And is well acquainted [with all things].[4]

It is significant that the latter verse is addressed to the whole of humankind, though the verses that precede this particular verse in the Quran are directed specifically to 'the believers'.[5] It can be argued, therefore, that the oneness of humankind is a truly universal concept which transcends not just the barriers of gender, language, community and nation but also surmounts the boundaries created by religion.

One of the best knwon *hadiths* (sayings) of the Prophet Muhammad lends forceful support to this non-sectarian perspective on the unity of humankind. In his farewell address during his last pilgrimage, he reiterated: 'All of you are from Adam and Adam was created from dust. An Arab is not superior to a non-Arab; neither is a white man superior to a black man, except on the basis of righteousness.[6]

If we reflect upon the philosophical basis of equality, it is apparent that there are various aspects to it. It is equality based upon a certain conception of man's nature, his humanity, his origin and his purpose. More than that, it is equality born of the oneness of the universal message, and therefore equality which repudiates all man-made dichotomies. Most of all, it is equality which derives its strength from its recognition of righteousness as the only factor that makes one human being unequal to another. And righteousness itself embodies faith in God and carrying out good deeds, which mean essentially helping the poor and needy, bringing freedom to others and proving one's honesty and sincerity.[7]

The sociological dimensions

This philosophical concept of equality finds specific meaning in various spheres. This is one of the unique attributes of Islam. However, in the process, certain changes have been wrought to the universal purity of the idea of equality, as we shall discover in a while.

In law, all persons are recognized as equal and 'entitled to equal opportunities and protection of the law'.[8] Similarly, all persons have the same right to a fair trial, and to protection against abuse of power and torture. At the same time, 'every persecuted or oppressed person has the right to seek refuge and asylum'.[9] It is significant that these rights are given to everyone, irrespective of sex, colour, ethnicity and religion.

However, Quranic law also makes some differentiation when it comes to women — a point which will be considered separately. Likewise, by placing the Muslims as a whole under a distinct legal system, the Sharia, it differentiates them from non-Muslims who may be living in the same country. This again will be discussed later when we consider ethnic relations in the context of equality.

In politics every person has equal right to freedom in all its forms, just as every person has the right to struggle against oppression, to protest against injustice and to criticize and correct the wrongdoings of those in power. Indeed, the Universal Islamic Declaration of Human Rights even asserts: 'It is the right and duty of every person to defend the rights of any other person and the community in general (*Hisbah*).'[10]

Among these rights is the right of a person to express his thoughts and beliefs and his right 'to participate individually and collectively in the religious, social, cultural and political life of his community'.[11] As part of this, Muslims and non-Muslims can choose, on their own free will, leaders to administer society on the basis of the Quran and Sunnah.

The core of the political and administrative leadership in a society guided by Islamic tenets should, however, comprise Muslim males who are devout and knowledgeable. This of course excludes both non-Muslims and women. The justifications given for this in Islamic thought will be spelt out in due course. Towards the end of this section we shall evaluate the legitimacy of these justifications.

For the time being, let us turn to economic rights in Islam. There is, on the whole, the same stress upon equality. Various ethical guidelines are provided to help man in his economic decisions and actions. By and large, the concern is with encouraging people to give and share rather than hoard and acquire.[12] This is why the resources of nature are seen as God's bounties meant for everyone. A contemporary document describes them as 'blessings bestowed by God for the benefit of Mankind as a whole'.[13] At the same time every person has the right to own property, individually or together with others. To ensure that this does not lead to inequalities, Islamic thinkers have suggested that all means of production should be used or controlled in the interest of the community. The religion also forbids usury, huge profits, monopolies and the like, with the aim of achieving equality. By the same token, Islam requires that workers are treated with utmost dignity.[14] It condemns exploitation and stipulates clearly that wages should be such that they would be sufficient to meet all basic needs. Indeed, providing food, clothes, shelter, medicine and employment is sometimes considered the responsibility of the community as a whole. Also, all persons are entitled to equal wages for equal work.

However, in spite of all these principles directed towards the quest of equality, the Quran appears to accept the poor as an inevitable element in the social panorama. It assumes that social disparities will always be there, and seeks to mitigate the effects of poverty by bestowing upon the poor the right to a prescribed share of the wealth of the rich through the institution of the *Zakat*.

In the relations between the sexes too there are traces of inequality just as there is also an undeniable commitment to equality. Women enjoy the same status as men when it comes to strictly spiritual matters — her prayer and her fast, for instance, have the same spiritual value as his. As human beings with a transcendental purpose which has to be realized through a life of righteousness, there is no differentiation in the position of the woman as against the man. Similarly, there is a clear recognition of the mutuality of rights and obligations. The Quran says, for instance, 'they are your garments and ye are their garments'.[15] It also notes that 'to men is allotted what they earn and to women what they earn. But ask Allah of His Bounty For Allah hath full knowledge of all things.'[16]

This equality is reflected in many specific spheres of human activity — at least as far as Islamic thought is concerned. A woman's labour has the same intrinsic value as a man's and has to be rewarded accordingly. Women can do whatever work is suitable for them as long as it is ethical and does not infringe upon their other roles as mothers and wives. They are entitled to own property, to engage in business on their own and to enter contracts in their own name. Education is a woman's right inasmuch as it is a man's. A woman can also participate in public affairs to some extent, provided that her role does not interfere with her more fundamental duties as mother and wife.

The woman's position in the home, either as mother or wife, is not the only basis for distinguishing her from the male. There is also the view that the woman is somehow the lesser of the sexes. The Quran itself maintains: 'And Women shall have rights similar to the rights Against them, according To what is equitable; But men have a degree [of advantage] over them And Allah is Exalted in Power, Wise.'[17]

In law and public affairs, as we have alluded, the lesser status of women becomes a little obvious. Her share of inheritance is less than the male's; her value as a witness is limited, compared to a male. It is generally accepted that she is temperamentally unsuited for certain public offices. Judgeship would be one of them. The leadership of government would be another. It has been argued that the physiological and psychological changes that women undergo during monthly periods and pregnancy affect their temperaments, and that leadership roles, 'require a maximum of rationality and a minimum of emotionality — a requirement which may not coincide with the instinctive nature of women'.[18]

With ethnic relations, the question of equality and inequality assumes yet another shade which makes the problem even more complex. Islam, as we have seen, acknowledges the common humanity of man. More than that we have been shown how by making righteousness, not religion, the criterion for differentiation between one person and another, Islam becomes truly universal in an all-transcending sense.

And yet, there is this idea of a separate unity among Muslims. The Quran, for instance, observes that 'The Believers are but A single Brotherhood: So make peace and Reconciliation between your Two (contending) brothers'.[19] While intra-religious unity of this type need not necessarily lead to chauvinism, it is nevertheless true that it creates a distinction of sorts.

Of course, the distinction in itself does not indicate any inequality. For non-Muslims enjoy equal and reciprocal rights and duties in most areas within an Islamic policy. These rights and duties are sanctified in Islamic legal theory by bestowing upon non-Muslims the title of *ahl al-dhimmah*, or 'those whose obligations are a trust upon the conscience and pledge of the state or the nation'.[20] The Charter of Medina drawn up by the Prophet Muhammad himself, his treaty with the Christians of Najran and the attitudes of the righteous caliphs were outstanding examples of tolerance and compassion towards non-Muslims.

The principles derived from this past allow non-Muslims to have their own laws based upon their own legal traditions or opt for the Sharia. They can preserve their own languages and cultures, practise their own religions, and perpetuate their own groups as distinct communities. They have every right to carry out their own economic activities with the full protection of the state. Non-Muslims are also entitled to participate in public affairs. They can comment upon any issue, including issues which are specific to Islam and the Muslim community, like the implementation of Islamic laws. They can help choose leaders for the state and can hold certain public offices. In this connection, non-Muslims can even sit in an Islamic legislature as representatives of non-Muslim interests.[21]

While all this is possible, non-Muslims, as we have noted earlier, cannot however perform any of the vital roles in the political and administrative set-up of an Islamic state. This would include serving as president, prime minister, a cabinet minister in a crucial Ministry, the head of the judiciary, the chief of the police or commander of the armed forces.

This exclusion would not be regarded as a form of discrimination by many Islamic political theorists, since policy formulation and leadership in an Islamic state should logically be in the hands of those who subscribe to that world-view. It would be the same in any social system guided by a particular social philosophy.

Reflections on equality

Before we reflect upon these sociological dimensions of equality in Islamic thought, it is necessary to clarify the status of the ideas expressed so far in relation to law, politics, economics, women and ethnicity. Most of the ideas belong to mainstream thinking on Islam. For in Islam, as in other belief systems, whether religious or secular, one should expect varied perspectives on philosophical ideas, especially when it involves a theme that is as complex as 'equality'. By selecting interpretations which can be traced back most easily to the Quranic revelation and the Sunnah, we have tried to evolve a view of equality which would represent the consensual middle. This does not mean, of course, that every interpretation on equality in this analysis has an unchallengeable Quranic base. Neither does it mean that there would be unanimous endorsement of the interpretations selected as reflective of consensual thinking on equality. Nevertheless, this perspective is, from the standpoint of an individual at least, an honest depiction of the general perception of what constitutes equality in Islamic thought.

It is apparent that while equality is the central concern of law, politics, economics, male–female relations and ethnic ties, there are also unmistakable elements of inequality. How does one explain the co-existence of what appear to be contradictory tendencies within the same doctrinal structure? Or are they, after all, part of one harmonious whole?

One can argue for instance that the so-called inequalities exist because of the natural state of affairs. As an example, men have to lead; women have secondary roles in certain areas. This is integral to God's plan. It is part of His perennial wisdom.

There is a flaw in this argument. We know that there is no natural law about man's leadership. Neither is it true that just because women are physically and temperamentally different they cannot lead society. Indeed, women are as rational or irrational as men are. They are capable of making judgements which are as sound as anything men are capable of. There is sufficient evidence to support this view of the female sex.[22]

Similarly, one cannot deny that emphasis upon unity within a particular religious community will eventually create an in-group–out-group dichotomy. This is inevitable since a grouping based upon a certain identity must mean the reinforcement of its sense of collective oneness through symbols, rituals and ceremonies. This must result in the erection of barriers between one group and the other.

This is why we find it difficult to understand how Muslim unity can contribute towards the universal brotherhood of man — which is the ultimate Islamic ideal. For the former means maintaining and perpetuating a particularistic tendency, the latter seeks to liberate the human being from all such tendencies so that he discovers his spiritual essence shorn of sectarian attachments.[23] It does not make sense, therefore, to pursue Muslim unity and universal brotherhood at the same time.

Besides, group identities must breed group interests. In fact, they reinforce each other. Confining certain leadership roles to one's own kind is part of this desire to protect the interests of the group. By so doing, one restricts — even if it is unconsciously done — the opportunities for others who are not part of the in-group to realize their full potentialities as human beings. What this means is that if one is convinced that it is righteous conduct, and not religious affiliation, that counts, then there is no justification to preserve certain positions for Muslims.[24] The same argument would apply with equal validity to the right of women to lead.

If sexual and ethnic inequalities have no basis, then neither does class inequality have basis. We have enough knowledge now of the possibilities of structural transformation to realize that poverty can be eradicated and social disparities eliminated if we pursue egalitarian policies formulated and implemented by honest, dedicated men and women. This is another way of saying that the rich–poor dichotomy is not eternal. Of course individual differences in attainment will always remain, but they need not — and should not — be allowed to develop into class divisions. In other words, with the growth of science and technology and the emphasis upon the masses in the restructuring of society, we do not have to require the rich to help the poor in order to achieve justice and equality. What this implies is that the institution of the *Zakat*, like the rules on inheritance or the prohibition on usury — just and wise as they are — cannot by themselves help to evolve a more equal social structure. And a truly equal society where 'Mankind is one nation' without being divided into classes is undoubtedly the aspiration of the Quran, viewed from its underlying philosophy.[25]

If that is the case, how does one explain those traces of inequality that we encountered? The explanation is perhaps related to the nature of the Quran and the character of its Divine Revelation. The Quran has a twofold purpose. First, it enunciates a universal message relevant for all times and pertinent to human beings in all circumstances. This it does by laying out eternal values and principles which one discovers through reflection and analysis of specific verses and the overall thrust of the Holy Book. Second, to make this exposition of a universal message meaningful to a particular people who had to practise it and, thereby, establish its validity for future generations, the Quran draws upon ideas and institutions, laws and lores which belonged to that specific, time-bound, place-bound context.

If anything, this testifies to God's infinite wisdom. For a universal truth would have lost its significance if it could not be transformed into a living truth demonstrated by a people operating within a particular setting. In the process of transformation, that universal truth takes on certain external features which may give the outward impression of distorting its inner qualities.

This is why if one studies the actual rules on inheritance, for instance, one realizes that some of the ideas makes sense only within the tribal-communal context of seventh-century Meccan society where the male had a dominant position. And yet the underlying emphasis even within that context is unambiguously clear — the aim is to achieve complete equality.

That equality of the sexes is the real goal becomes obvious when one examines the status of women in that society during that period in relation to the far-reaching reforms affected by the Quran. A thing like the woman's position as a witness in judicial matters will be seen in a different light when one realizes that all the changes to her status brought about by Islam were so fundamental that it transformed the entire value system of the Arab male for a few decades. Indeed, as far as the position of women goes, there is no denying that the spirit of the Quranic message is irrevocably committed to liberation.[27] It is the failure of succeeding generations to continue with the reforms — to transform the spirit of the message into the letter of the law — that one should condemn.

Similarly, one understands why Muslim unity is given some significance in certain parts of the Quran. A new community had just come into being. It was under siege, threatened by more powerful forces without any moral scruples. Unity became imperative to defend the integrity, indeed to ensure the very survival, of the nascent Muslim community.

But more important, the community was expected to embody the great virtues contained in the Quran. To preserve those virtues, it had to establish its own separate identity; it had to distinguish itself from the corruption and decadence of the surrounding milieu. The call to unity must be viewed within that context. That what was intended was essentially a unity of virtues was obvious from the Quranic warning that even among the believers the evil would be separated from the good.[28] This harmonizes well with the notion of righteousness — that is, devotion to God and good deeds — which, as we have shown, is the only criterion for distinguishing one human being from another.

The preservation of certain leadership roles for Muslims should also be evaluated against this background. The real purpose was the protection of certain righteous qualities, particularly vital in the context of the struggle that was taking place at that time. The Quran does not say that Muslims are entitled to certain positions simply because they are Muslims. That would be against the entire spirit of the Quran. For the Quran places so much emphasis upon the actual deed, rather than the professed word, in judging human beings. Besides, it sees the strengths and weaknesses of human character as applicable to all groups and communities. There is nothing in the Quran to suggest that Muslims are exempt from the laws of human behaviour — or the laws of history. This is why claiming an exclusive role, preserving a privileged position for oneself by virtue of one's professed faith is certainly a betrayal of the tone and tenor of the Quran.

There is perhaps no greater authoritative support for this than the writings of that illustrious savant, Abul Kalam Azad. Azad was convinced that the Quran did not intend to create an exclusive religion. Its only goal is the unity of man. As he put it,

> no other truth of the Quran has been kept so deliberately out of sight than this. Should one study the Quran with an open mind, with every predilection strictly kept aside, and look into its numerous clear assertions in this respect, and then look at those who nevertheless regard the religion of the Quran as nothing else than an exclusive religious groupism, even as other religions, one will assuredly cry out that either the eyes of such people deceive them or that they deliver their verdict on anything even without looking at it.[29]

Just as Muslims have come to wrong conclusions about religious exclusivism without comprehending the real meaning of the Quran, so they have failed to appreciate why the spirit of the Quran is against class divisions. Without any doubt at all, the spirit behind the *Zakat*, the inheritance laws, the prohibition of usury, monopolies and so on is the quest for equality. However, within the context of a largely tribal, pre-modern society whose economy was dominated by merchant capital this could only express itself through various exhortations and injunctions against the accumulation of wealth. Here again, the underlying motive of controlling the rich, of dividing property equitably, of raising the status of the poor should have inspired latter-day Muslims to institute fundamental changes — changes which would have brought them closer to their ideal of an egalitarian society.

So strong is this ideal in the religion that a contemporary Muslim scholar has argued that in Islam, 'All realities are on the same level. No top and no base. No higher and no lower. Transporting this linear concept of human life, we will have a society without classes. All members of this society are equal. The horizontal dimension of life not the vertical one is history.'[30]

To arrive at such an interpretation of what equality means in Islam, it is apparent that one has to emphasize the underlying spirit rather than particular verses. The importance of doing this is perhaps best demonstrated by examining briefly yet another spiritual value — freedom. That the Quran advocates human freedom is an understatement. Nearly every major idea or episode in it is somehow related to the question of freedom, from man's creation, to the exercise of free will as man's unique gift from God, to his position as the vice-regent of God, to the plea to uphold freedom of speech and association, and finally to the call to enjoin what is good and forbid what is wrong. And yet there is no specific verse in the Quran that prohibits slavery — though there is outright banning of other forms of social evil. In spite of this no one who has studied the Quran will deny that Islam is against slavery. The encouragement to free slaves, the advice to treat slaves as if they were part of one's own family, apart from the Quranic commitment to freedom are all evidence to show where the religion stands on this question. Of course, slavery could not be abolished that easily because it was one of the pillars on which the economic edifice of Meccan society rested. But the Quran indicates nevertheless, through the overall thrust of its message, the illegitimacy of the institution. This is why a philosophical understanding of the deeper meaning of the Quran is imperative.

The validity of such an approach is suggested by the Quran itself. If we reflect upon the verses revealed at Mecca we will notice that they are, on the whole, more directly universal, more concerned with the general human condition. The verses revealed at Medina, on the other hand, are much more specific and deal with particular situations and specific circumstances.[31] This is understandable, for during his Meccan years Muhammad's sacred mission was to disseminate the universal truth about *Tauhid* (the oneness of God), the central doctrine of Islam, and all that it implies in terms of spiritual values. In Medina, he had to govern a community — the first Muslim community — and God's guidance therefore dealt with the specific issues of law, politics and the economy. It goes without saying that unless one is able to derive universal principles from these particular injunctions, one will not understand why it is said that Islam is applicable to all times and all places.

Equality: progressive and conservative perspectives

What all this shows is that in Islam it is possible to develop a perspective on equality which is far more progressive than even the consensual middle would allow. At the same time, yet another approach could result in a conservative conception of equality which is more retrogressive than provided for by the consensual middle.

In order to obtain a clearer understanding of all the examples we have given of how equality can be linked to the underlying spirit of the Quran, it is necessary to elaborate some of the characteristics of a progressive perspective on Islam. They will be contrasted with some of the features of conservative Islam.

First — and perhaps most obvious of all — progressive Islam emphasizes the spirit rather than the details contained in the scriptures of the religion. It is the underlying philosophy that it cherishes most, the reasoning, the thinking, the emotion behind a particular instruction or prohibition.

Second, this means that the historical, sociological context of the divine teachings and of the mission of the Prophet Muhammad would be taken into account in any endeavour to understand the values and principles of Islam. It must be emphasized that this is in no way a repudiation of the Quran's, or even the Sunnah's, eternal, universal significance. It cannot be. For by separating the contextual from the perennial one would be reinforcing faith in the unchanging fundamentals. In that way, some of the doubts and uncertainties about the validity of certain practices in the religion which have often plagued modern Muslim minds would be overcome.

Third, the moment one emphasizes the spirit of Islam, on the one hand, and acknowledges the importance of the sociological dimension in the analysis of the philosophy of the religion, on the other, one begins to see Islam as an evolutionary, dynamic movement through time. It ceases to be a revelation whose universality and perenniality were established in an immutable form at a certain point in history. Islam becomes a continuous unfolding, an unceasing process which seeks rejuvenation from age to age through the absorption of new knowledge.[32]

Fourth, the absorption of new knowledge must necessarily lead to an active dialogue with other intellectual traditions. It must mean a willingness to allow new ideas and values to shape and mould the eternal truths in the religion.

Finally, as important as dialogue with other intellectual traditions is constant interaction with other spiritual traditions. Progressive Islam would place a high premium on this, for it recognizes that God is one and Truth is indivisible. It would even acknowledge that in their concept of good deeds, in their perception of good values, in their vision of the meaning and purpose of life, and indeed in their view of the ultimate reality (especially the mystical perspective on this) all the great religions share many common positions.

All these attributes of progressive Islam are absent in the conservative conception of Islam. In a nutshell, it is an Islam that is obsessed with scriptural details, that negates reason and reflection, that is opposed to distinguishing the contextual from the perennial, that refuses to admit fresh currents of thought, that denies the need for interaction with other religions, that encourages, if unwittingly, static, fixed attitudes and beliefs which in reality repudiate universal truths.

It is a tragedy that conservative Islam has a greater hold upon the Muslim mind than progressive Islam at this stage in history. Why this is so lies outside the scope of this chapter. Suffice it to say that the consolidation of hereditary power, class stratification, the country–city dichotomy, the destruction of the major centres of Islamic civilization in the Middle Ages, the onslaught of colonialism, the unequal distribution of either wealth or political power or both in many post-colonial Muslim states, and the continued existence of an unequal international system have all contributed towards the emergence and perpetuation of conservative Islam.

Conclusion

It is only too apparent that liberation from conservative Islam is vital for the future of Muslims everywhere. But progressive Islam can triumph only if the various forces which keep conservative Islam ascendent — forces which we mentioned earlier — are totally defeated.

It is in this connection that the quest for equality is important because more than anything else, this quest has compelled Muslims to reappraise class, community and sex relations to find out to what extent Islam seeks equality. And since the quest for equality is one of those irreversible trends in human history, it is quite conceivable that it will continue to challenge existing structures and attitudes within the Muslim world, as elsewhere. In the process, we may witness one of the major transformations in Islamic thought — a transformation which will finally bestow supreme significance upon one of its most cherished values.

Notes

Abbreviations

The following is a list of abbreviations of sources used in the Notes.

A, A.N.   Anguttara Nikāya
B.G.   Bhagavad gītā
Bṛhad   Bṛhad-Āraṇyaka Upaniṣad
Chānd.   Chāndogya Upaniṣad
D.   Dīgha Nikāya
Dh.S.   Dharma Śāstra
Kaush.   Kaushītaki Upaniṣad
Mah.   Mahābhārata
Maj.   Majjhima Nikāya
Mund.   Muṇḍaka Upaniṣad
R.V.   Ṛg Veda
S.N.   Sutta Nipāta
Svetas   Śvetāśvatara Upaniṣad
Taitt.   Taittirīya Upaniṣad

Equality and inequality in the Hindu scriptures

1. 'Bhavatyadharmo dharma hi dharmādharmavubhavapi Kāranāddesakālasya desakālah Sa tādṛsaḥ' (Mahābhārata, Śāntiparva, 78.32).
2. 'Dharmā-rtha-kāma-mokṣānāmupadeśasamanvitaṃ Pūrvavṛttaṃ kathāyuktam itihāsam pracakṣyate' (V.S. Apte, The Practical Sanscrit English Dictionary, p. 254).
3. 'Naiva rājyaṃ rājāsīnna ca daṇḍo na daṇḍikah dharmeṇa vaiprājah sarva rakṣanti sma parasparaṃ' (Mahābhārata, Śāntiparva, 58.14).
4. The ten kinds of Brāhmaṇas referred to in the Haśabrāhmana Jataka (III, pp. 2090–1) are: tikicchākasamā, Paricārakasama, niggāhaka, khānugghāta, Vanijaka, Ambathavessehi, goghataka, gopanisadehi, Luddaka and Malamjanasamā.
5. 'Śrenyo rajakādyastādaśa hīnajātayaḥ'. (Quoted by Kane, History of Dharmasaśtra vol. II, Part 1, p. 70).

Equality and inequality in the religious and cultural traditions of Hinduism and Buddhism

1. E.A. Burtt, 'A Basic Problem in the Quest for Understanding between East and West' in Charles Moor, ed., *Philosophy and Culture—East and West* (Honolulu: University of Hawaii Press, 1968), p. 677.
2. B. Heimann, Facets of Indian Thought (London: George Allen & Unwin Ltd., 1964), pp. 49–60.
3. International Encyclopaedia for the Social Sciences, vols. 5 and 6 (New York: Macmillan and Free Press, 1977), p. 108.
4. J. Muir, *Original Sanskrit Texts*, vol. 1 (Amsterdam: Oriental Press, 1967), 2nd edn, p. 240.
5. Ibid., p. 245.
6. Ibid., p. 262.
7. Ibid., p. 258.
8. Ibid., p. 280.
9. J.N. Farquhar, *An Outline of the Religious Literature of India* (Oxford: Oxford University Press, 1920), p. 5.
10. R.V. (VI.44. 11).
11. Ibid. (VIII.53.1).
12. Ibid. (I.72.5)
13. Ibid. (I.83.3).
14. Ibid. (I.131.3 and VIII.131.5).
15. Ibid. (X.115.3).
16. Ibid. (VIII.38.17).
17. Ibid. (X.96.15).
18. Ibid. (V.61.6).
19. However see W.D. O'Flaherty, *Women, Androgynes and Other Mythical Beasts* (Chicago, University of Chicago Press; 1980), p. 32. Here it is evident that in regard to the androgyne, although the male and female elements are more or less equal, the male is 'more equal' than the female. Also see pp. 47–8 on the retention of milk and seed for a continuation of this theme.
20. This is clearly evident in the Soma hymns of the ninth book of the *Ṛg Veda*, where the hymns are specifically for the use of the *udgatṛ* only. See. A.A. Macdonell, *A Vedic Reader* (Madras, Oxford University Press, 1965), p. xv.
21. M. Winternitz, *Die Frau in den indischen Religionen* (Leipzig: Verlag von Curt Kabitzch, 1920), pp. 57–9 and p. 82.
22. It is significant that we have evidence of prescribed rites for the birth of a daughter only in Upaniṣadic texts and not earlier. In the Veda there are hymns expressing prayers to the gods for sons, but not for daughters, and this attitude can be seen in the Brahmanic texts too.
23. M. Winternitz, *Die Frau in den indischen Religionen*, p. 121. 'Nowhere so clearly as in Brahminism is it shown that the woman was always the best friend of religion, but religion was by no means a friend of the woman' (author's translation).
24. Kaṭha. (2.16.), Maitri (4.4.), Muṇḍ. (1.1.5).

25. Chānd. (6.1.1–3.).
26. Muṇḍ. (1.2.7.).
27. Bṛhad. (2.4.1–14). Also see Chānd. (4.4.4.) where Satyakāma Jabala who does not know of what family he is, is welcomed as a student of sacred knowledge. (Reference to him as a 'Brahman' is comparable to the identification of a Brahman in Buddhism).
28. Kaṭha (1.21.) and (5.12.).
29. Bṛhad. (1.4.10.).
30. Ibid. (4.5.1.).
31. Chānd. (3.5.2.).
32. Kaṭha (1.1.).
33. Chānd. (3.11.5.). See also Śvetāś. (6.22) where 'The supreme mystery in the Vedas end should not be given to one who is not tranquil, nor again to one who is not a son or a pupil'.
34. Kaush. (2.15.) See also Chānd, (1.5.2.) on the desire for sons and Bṛhad. (1.5.17.), for their value.
35. Bṛhad. (4.5).
36. 'There is no difference here at all: He goes from death to death Who seems to see a difference here' (Katha. 4.11.).
37. Bṛhad. (1.3.22).
38. Taitt. (3.7–10).
39. Here I am mainly concerned with the beliefs found in early Buddhist thought and not with later Mahāyānist developments.
40. M. Winternitz, *A History of Indian Literature* vol. 1 (Calcutta University Press, 1933.), pp. 236 ff. The age of a particular *Upaniṣad* may be determined by the language used. A.B. Keith in *The Religion and Philosophy of the Veda and Upanishads* (Cambridge, Mass.: Harvard University Press and London: Oxford University Press, 1925), pp. 501–2 says that it is very difficult to ascertain which *Upaniṣads* were pre- and which post-Buddhist. I think that it would be inaccurate to dismiss the likelihood of Upaniṣadic influences on early Buddhist texts and vice versa. Both the *Upaniṣads* and Buddhist texts make a significant break away from the traditional Brahmanical ritual and class order; both show a new respect for the mental capacity of the individual; both encourage the participation of women in spiritual discussions and both give a similar and new significance to the concept of *karma*.
41. *Aggañña Sutta* (D. 111. 85–6).
42. Cf. Bṛhad. (1.4.14.): 'He (Brahma) created still further a better form, Law (*dharma*). This is the power (*kṣatra*), of the Kshatriya class viz. Law. Therefore there is nothing higher than Law. So a weak man controls a strong man by Law, just as if by a king. Verily, that which is Law is truth. Therefore they say of a man who speaks the truth, "He speaks the Law"; or of a man who speaks the Law, "He speaks the truth". Verily both these are the same thing.' The reference here to the *Kshatriya* class is probably because the creators of the texts were showing an attitude to an existing class order. The content of the Upaniṣadic passage differs from the Buddhist passage mainly in the former's categorization of gods, but not specifically with regard to the nature of *dharma* or its importance for the king.

43. *Digha Nikaya Aṭṭhakatha*, III. P.T.S., p. 850, quoted by K.N. Jayatileke in *The Principles of International Law in Buddhist Doctrine* (Leyden: A.W. Sijthoft).

44. The *Dhammapada*, Verse 393.

45. *Vāseṭṭhasutta* (S.N. 601–11).

46. *Vasalasutta* (S.N. 135).

47. See *Ambattasutta* (D. 111.1.), where 'The Kshatriya is the best of these among folk who put their trust in lineage. But he who is perfect in wisdom and righteousness, he is the best among gods and men'. Also the *Aggañña Sutta* (D.111. 5–6), the *Kannakatthala Sutta*, the *Madhura Sutta* (Maj. 84), and the *Aśśalāyana Sutta* (Maj. 93). In the *Madhura* and *Aśśalāyana suttas*, the Buddha maintains that all humans may serve or be served, be moral or immoral, dress in saffron robes and choose the homeless life regardless of caste, and that ultimately a distinction can only be made on ethical grounds.

48. Piyadassi Thera, *The Virgin's Eye* (Colombo: Buddhist Publication Society, 1980), pp. 33–52.

49. *Samyutta Nikāya* (III.2.6.).

50. (A.N. III. 37–8, IV. 265) as quoted by I.B. Horner in *Women in Early Buddhist Literature* (Kandy: Buddhist Publication Society, 1978), pp. 14–15.

51. *Anguttara Nikāya Book of the Fours* (X.80). Here *sabhā* could mean an assembly. J. Dhirasekara has indicated to me that by examining the commentarial tradition, the word *kamboja*, a place name, has been wrongly transliterated into the Sinhalese script as *kammojam* from the original.

52. We do have an example of the maiden Kāśisundarī who had to change her sex before becoming an arahant in the *Suvarnavaṇavādāna*. This text may be dated to AD 300 or 400. See 'Suvarnavanavādāna, translated and edited together with its Tibetan translation and the Laksacaityasamutpatti' (thesis submitted for the degree of Doctor of Philosophy of the Australian National University by T. Rajapatirana, p. 54.

53. *Avaivartika* implies that there could be a rank of Bodhisattva capable of sliding back, and from the context, we may say that females could fall into the latter, more inferior category. It has been noted that the beings mentioned here all appear in the Sanskrit in the masculine gender. This may be contrasted to the Śvetāmbara sect of Jainism which was roughly contemporary to Buddhism and claimed that the Tīrthankara Malli was female. Tārā and other goddesses are sometimes referred to as having the 'rank of Bodhisattva'; see A. Getty, *The Gods of Northern Buddhism*, (Oxford: Clarendon Press, 1914), pp. 103ff. It is likely that the goddess did not acquire this status in her own right, but rather as a consort of a Bodhisattva, or as the emanation of a Buddha. It is possible that she acquired this status through recognition first as a goddess, at a time when the concept of deity and Bodhisattva was almost indistinguishable in later, Sanskrit Buddhist texts.

54. Nancy Schuster, 'Changing the Female Body: Wise Women and the Bodhisattva Career in Some Maharatnakutasutras', *Journal of the International Association of Buddhist Studies*, vol. 4, no. 1, 1981, pp. 24–69, indi-

cates that a certain asexuality is evident in the changing of the body. However she appears only to refer to the changing of the female to the male body and not vice versa. This implies that the male body is either the norm, or the superior spiritual form, which is indicative of inequality.

55.   E.J. Thomas, *The Life of the Buddha as Legend and History* (London: Routledge, 1949), p. 107. J. Dhirasekara, *Buddhist Monastic Discipline* (Colombo, Sri Lanka: Ministry of Higher Education Research Publication Series, 1982), has pointed out that this hesitation of the Buddha was because he was aware of the laxity in the behaviour of male and female mendicants of the time. It is also possible that the Buddha preferred not to contribute to changing women's social position by taking her away from her more usual role, within the household.

56.   I.B. Horner, *Women under Primitive Buddhism* (London: Routledge and Sons Ltd., 1930) p. 119, has indicated that most of the sayings which have been attributed to the Buddha were edited by monks, and that it is not unlikely that they might have attempted to minimize the importance of women in their writings. However, the mentioned passages as they appear to us today remain without alteration, and have not been denied by later texts, so their validity in Theravāda Buddhism cannot be overlooked. The Buddhist attitude to nuns is comparable to the Digambara attitude, where nuns are technically of a lower rank than monks; but in the latter case, it is because nuns (unlike monks) cannot enter into ascetic nudity. However in the Śvetāmbara and Sthānakavāsi, which are Jain sects, nuns and monks take the same vows and are considered as spiritual equals. See P. Jaini, *The Jaina Path of Purification* (Berkeley: University of California Press, 1979), p. 246.

57.   It has to be noted that in rural Buddhist India, women were often found working, and that it was only women of a certain social class and background who did not work. This is probably more on account of economic necessity than specifically of Buddhist religious influence. In urban and noble families which were economically self sufficient, the women usually worked within the home carrying out administrative as well as domestic duties, as is in keeping with the Buddhist texts that have come down to us today.

58.   The *Bhagavad-gītā*, tr. S. Radhakrishnan, p. 14.

59.   'For those who take refuge in Me, O Partha (Arjuna) though they are lowly born, women, Vaisyas as well as Sudras, they also attain to the highest goal' (ibid. IX.32).

60.   Ibid., II.47.

61.   Ibid., V.18–19.

62.   Ibid., VI.9.

63.   Ibid., IX.23.

64.   Ibid., XI.52.

65.   K. Subramanium, *The Mahābhārata* (Bombay: Bharatiya Vidya Bhavan, 1980), p. 44.

66.   Ibid., LIX.111–13.

67.   Ibid., LXXXX1.5.

68. A.A. Macdonell, *A History of Sanskrit Literature* (London: William Heinemann, 1900), p. 428.

69. J.J. Meyer, *Das Weib im altindischen Epos* (Leipzig: Verlag von Wilhem Heims, 1915), pp. 307–9.

70. E.W. Hopkins, 'The Status of Women in the epics', *Journal of the American Oriental Society*, vol. 13, 1887, p. 330.

71. Mahābhārata, I.157.37, as quoted by Hopkins, 'The Status of Women', p. 340.

72. Hopkins, 'The Status of Women', p. 349.

73. Ibid. p. 364.

74. A.L. Basham, *The Wonder that was India* (London: Fortuna, 1977), p. 118.

75. Ibid. p. 121.

76. E.W. Hopkins 'Ancient and Modern Hindu Gilds', *Yale Review*, May and August, 1898, pp. 24–5.

77. Vaśishtha, Dh. S. (XXVIII.2–3), quoted in S.R. Shastri, *Women in 'the Sacred Laws'* (Bombay: Bharatiya Vidya Bhavan: 1959), p. 46.

78. Manu (IV. 185.) quoted in Shastri, *Women in 'the Sacred Laws'*.

79. J.D.M. Derrett, *Religion, Law and the State in India* (London: Faber and Faber, 1968), p. 169.

80. I.C. Sharma, 'Human Rights and Comprehensive Humanism' in A.S. Rosenbaum, ed., *The Philosophy of Human Rights; International Perspectives*, (Westport, Conn., Greenwood Press, 1980). pp. 103–12.

The concept of equality in the Therevāda Buddhist tradition

1. Adamantia Pollis and Peter Schwab, 'Human Rights: A Western Construct with Limited Applicability' in Pollis and Schwab, eds. *Human Rights* (New York, 1979), p. 1.

2. See, L. M. Joshi, *Aspects of Buddhism in Indian History* (Kandy: Buddhist Publication Society, 1973).

3. Ibid.

4. Buddhist traditions may be divided into three forms: (i) the Theravāda (meaning the teaching of the elders), found in the South-east Asia region, Sri Lanka, Burma, and Thailand, as well as in Laos, Vietnam and Cambodia; (ii) The Mahāyāna (meaning the Great Vehicle), found in Nepal, China, Korea and Japan; (iii) the Tantrayāna (the esoteric vehicle), found in Tibet, Mongolia and parts of Siberia.

5. Joshi, *Aspects of Buddhism in Indian History*, p. 8.

6. Ninian Smart, *Worldviews: Cross-cultural Explorations of Human Beliefs*, (New York, 1983).

7. Ibid.

8. SN, 1, 99.

9. *Majjhima-Nikāya*, Sutta 136

10. SN, 136, 142.

11. See, Soma Thera, tr., *Kālāma Sutta*, (Kandy: Buddhist Publication Society, 1959).

12. O. H. de A. Wijesekera, *Buddhism and Society*, (Colombo; Bauddha Sahitya Sabha Publication); also see, D III, 59.
13. See S. Tachibana, *The Ethics of Buddhism* (Colombo, 1943).
14. *Dīgha-Nikāya*, Sutta 31.
15. For an interesting discussion of this point and for the reference to the *Li-chi*, see A.S. Cua, 'Li and Moral Justification: A Study in Li Chi', *Philosophy East and West*, January 1983.
16. Ibid.
17. D 1, 89.
18. Bernard Williams, 'The Idea of Equality' in Joel Feinberg, ed., *Moral Concepts* (Oxford: Oxford University Press, 1972), p. 155.
19. It is interesting to note that in recent studies of caste in India, the concept of social mobility has received considerable attention: 'Historically, the Kshatriya Varna was recruited from a wide variety of castes all of which had one attribute in common, that is, the possession of political power.' 'When a leader of a dominant caste or small chieftan graduated to the position of a raja or king, acquiring in the process the symbolic and other appurtenances of kshatriyahood, he in turn became a source of mobility for individuals and groups living in this domain. A necessary concommitant, if not a pre-condition, of such graduation was Sanskritization, that is, the acceptance of the rites, beliefs, ideas and values of the great tradition of Hinduism as embodied in Sacred Books.' M. N. Srinivasan, 'Mobility in the Caste System' in Milton Singer and Bernard S. Cohn, eds, *Structure and Change in Indian Society* (Illinois, 1968), pp. 189–99.
20. See T.W. Rhys Davids, tr., *Dialogues of the Buddha* (London: Luzac and Co. Ltd., 1956), p. 105.
21. *Digha-Nikaya*, Sutta 27.
22. *Ibid*. Sutta 26.
23. D. III, 83.
24. G.P. Malalasekera and K.N. Jayatilleke, *Buddhism and the Race Question* (Paris: Unesco, 1958), p. 20: Also see, K.N. Jayatilleke, *The Principles of Law in Buddhist Doctrine* (The Hague: 1967). Also, some relevant discussion is found in the unpublished papers submitted by the 'Buddhist Group' for the Human Rights Seminar, held in Colombo at the Sri Lanka Foundation Institute in 1981.
25. For a discussion of the Buddhist attitude to religious pluralism, see Padmasiri de Silva, 'Religious Pluralism: A Buddhist Perspective' in John Hick and Hasan Askari, *ed.*, *The Experience of Religious Diversity* (London, in press).
26. James Hastins (ed.), *Encyclopedia of Religion and Ethics*, (Edinburgh/London: T. and T. Clark, 1937), vol. 5, p. 276.
27. Padmasiri de Silva, *Buddhist and Freudian Psychology* (Colombo, 1973, p. 78).
28. See, Padmasiri de Silva, *Tangles and Webs* (Colombo, 1978, p. 76).
29. Cūlavagga.
30. Kajiyama Yuichi, 'Women in Buddhism', *The Eastern Buddhist*, Autumn, 1982, p. 60.
31. Ibid.
32. *Majjhima-Nikāya*, Sutta 115.

33. AN, 1, 15.
34. See, I.B. Horner, *Women under Primitive Buddhism* (London, 1930); I.B. Horner, *Women in Early Buddhist Literature* (Kandy: Buddhist Publication Society, 1978); Helmuth Hecker, *Buddhist Women at the Time of the Buddha* (Kandy: Buddhist Publication Society, 1982).
35. See H.N.S. Karunatilleke, *This Confused Society* (Colombo, 1976); E.F. Schumacher, *Small is Beautiful* (London, 1973); Padmasiri de Silva, 'Basic Needs and the Ethic of Restraint', paper presented to the Conference of World Buddhist Scholars and Leaders in Colombo, in July 1982.
36. D III, 61.
37. For the distinction between the 'dilemmatic' and the 'diagnostic' in the Buddhist context, see Padmasiri de Silva, 'Buddhism and the Tragic Sense of Life', *University of Ceylon Review*, April and October, 1967: 'Why do men get into problematic situations, is a more important question than how can we resolve this particular dilemma.'
38. We have attempted in this paper to explore the specific variables in the Buddhist world-view which colour its perspective on the equality concept and thus emphasize a non-Western vision of man and polity. But in cross-cultural studies we discover interesting points of convergence, too. In this context the recent work of John Rawls on 'Justice' and its implications for equality notions offers a strange sense of topicality to the Buddhist concept of righteousness, especially in its expressions as equity, impartiality and fairness. Rawls gives a key place to the notion of fairness: see John Rawls, 'The Sense of Justice' in Joel Feinberg, ed., *Moral Concepts* (Oxford, Oxford University Press, 1972).
39. Peter K.Y. Woo, 'A Metaphysical Approach to Human Rights from a Chinese point of view', in Allan Rosenbaum, ed., *The Philosophy of Human Rights: International Perspectives*, (Westport, Conn., Greenwood Press, 1980), p. 115.
40. Carol Gilligan, *In a Different Voice* (New York, 1983).
41. Ibid, p. 19.
42. Ibid, pp. 164–5.

The radical egalitarianism of Mahāyāna Buddhism

1. See Max Weber, *The Religions of India: The Sociology of Hinduism and Buddhism* (Boston: Beacon Press, 1959).
2. See, for instance, Susan B. Naquin, *Millenarian Rebellion in China* (New Haven: Yale University Press, 1976); and Daniel L. Overmyer, *Folk Buddhism in China* (Cambridge, Mass.: Harvard University Press, 1977).
3. I.B. Horner, ed. and tr., *The Collection of Middle Length Sayings* (Majjhima Nikāya), 3 vols. (London: Luzac and Co. for the Pali Text Society, 1967), vol. 3 pp. 147–52 and 153–62.
4. Specifically, the conditioned process of cognition moves through the five *khandas* or aggregates: (1) the sense organs of hearing, seeing, smelling, touching, and so on, come into contact with phenomenal objects produc-

ing (2) feeling which generates a (3) perception which in turn is conditioned by (4) volition and then acted upon by (5) consciousness.

5. James B. Pratt, *The Pilgrimage of Buddhism* (New York: The Macmillan Co., 1928, pp. 235–7.

6. D.T. Suzuki, *Outlines of Mahāyāna Buddhism* (London: Luzac and Co., 1907), p. 173.

7. Th. Stcherbatsky, *The Conception of Nirvana* (Leningrad: Institute for Cultural Studies 1927), p. 42.

8. D.T. Suzuki, ed. and tr., *Awakening of Faith* (Chicago: Open Court Publishers, 1900), pp. 77–8.

9. For Theravadins, *tathāgata* is translated as 'the-one-thus-gone'.

10. Edward J. Thomas, *History of Buddhist Thought* (London: Routledge and Kegan Paul, 1953), p. 234.

11. For the complete translation of the *Vimilakīrti Nirdesa Sūtra*, see H. Idumi, tr. 'Vimilakîrti's Discourse on Emancipation' in *Eastern Buddhist*, vol. 3, 1924–5, pp. 55–69, 138–53, 224–42 and 336–49, and vol. 4, 1926–8, pp. 48–55, 177–90 and 348–66.

12. Shunryu Suzuki, *Zen Mind, Beginner's Mind* (New York: John Weatherhill, Inc., 1981), p. 21.

13. Heinrich Dumoulin, *A History of Zen Buddhism* (Boston: Beacon Press, 1969), pp. 80–90.

14. David Kinsley, *The Sword and the Flute* (Berkeley: University of California Press, 1975), p. 120.

15. Caps, Mine and Dumoulin *op cit.* pp. 112–17.

Conceptions of equality and human nature in Taoism

1. Yoshimi Murakami, 'Kaku Shō no sisō ni tsuite' (On the Philosophy of Kuo Hsiang), *Tōyōshi Kenkyu*, vol. 6, no. 3, 1963.

2. *Tao-te-ching of Lao-tsu*, tr. J.L.L. Duyvendak (London: John Murray, 1954).

3. Karl Jaspers, *Konfuzius, Laotse* (Kōshi to Rōshi), tr. Gen. Tanaka, (Tokyo, 1967).

4. Max Weber, *Konfuzianismus und Taoismus* (Jukyō to dōkyō), tr. Tokuo Kimata, (Tokyo, 1971).

5. Yoshimi Murakami, 'Nature in Lao–Chuang Thought and "No–Mind" in Ch'an Buddhism', Kwansei Gakuin University, 1965 (unpublished).

7. Sun Wen (Chung-shan), *San-min chu-i* (Tokyo: Kaizō bunko, 1929).

8. Yoshimi Murakami, 'Affirmation of Desire in Taoism', *Acta Asiatica*, Vol. 27, 1974, pp. 57–74.

9. Yoshimi Murakami, *Rikuchō shisōshi kenkyū* (Studies in Six Dynasties Thought), (Kyoto, 1974).

10. Yoshimi Murakami, 'Shiyu ho Tai' (Tzu-yu's Visit to Tai), *Festschrift für Mori Mikisaburō* (Tokyo, 1978).

11. Taichiro Kobayashi, *Geijutsu no rikai no tame ni* (Towards an Understanding of Art), (Tokyo, 1960).

The concept of equality in Islamic thought

1. It is often referred to as Ad–Din, or the way of life suitable to man's nature. For a fuller analysis see Mawlana Abdul Kalam Azad, *The Tarjumanal-Quran*, vol. 1, tr. Dr Syed Abdul Latif (Lahore, 1968), especially section VII.
2. There is a brilliant exposition of the spiritually guided creative evolution of life in the Quran in Maurice Bucaille, *What is the Origin of Man?* (Paris: Seghers, 1982).
3. See Abdullah Yusuf Ali, *The Holy Quran*, text, translation and commentary (Lahore: Sh. Muhammad Ashraf, 1972), Sura II: 213.
4. Ibid, Sura XLIX: 13.
5. Ibid, XLIX: 10, 11 and 12.
6. This message is quoted in various texts with slight variations. See for instance, M. Aman Hobohm, 'Islam and the Racial Problem', in Altaf Gauhar, ed., *The Challenge of Islam* (London: Islamic Council of Europe, 1978), p. 275.
7. This idea is expressed in Kalam Azad, *Tarjumanal-Quran*, p. 159.
8. See *Universal Islamic Declaration of Human Rights* (London: Islamic Council of Europe, September, 1981), p. 7.
9. Ibid, p. 9.
10. Ibid, p. 8.
11. Ibid, p. 11.
12. These values are well articulated in Sayyid Qutb, *Social Justice in Islam* (Washington, 1953).
13. See *Universal Islamic Declaration*, p. 11.
14. See various essays in Hobohm, *The Challenge of Islam*, including Mouloud Kassim Nait-Belkacem, 'The Concept of Social Justice in Islam'; A.K. Brohi 'Islam & Human Rights'; and Khurshid Ahmad, 'Islam and the Challenge of Economic Development'.
15. See Yusuf Ali, *The Holy Quran*, Sura II: 187.
16. Ibid, Sura IV: 32.
17. Ibid, Sura II: 228.
18. See Gamal A. Badawi 'Woman in Islam', in Khurshid Ahmad, ed., *Islam — its Meaning and Message* (London: Islamic Council of Europe, 1976) p. 143. See also M. Mazheruddin Siddiqi, *Women in Islam* (Lahore: Institute of Islamic Culture, 1979).
19. See Yusuf Ali, *The Holy Quran*, Sura XLIX: 10.
20. See, for instance, Said Ramadan, *Islamic Law, its Scope and Equity* (Geneva: Said Ramadan, 1970), p. 122 for some reflections.
21. See A. A. Maududi, *Islamic Law and Constitution*, ed. and tr. Khurshid Ahmad (Lahore: Islamic Publications, 1960), for a detailed exposition of the position of non-Muslim minorities in an Islamic state.
22. This is the sane, rational position associated with some of the best thinkers on the female question. For an early analysis on this see, for instance, Simone de Beauvoir, *The Second Sex* (New York: Vintage Books, 1974).
23. This universalism in Islam is stressed by certain writers, among them Ali Shariati, *On the Sociology of Islam*, tr. Hamid Algar (Berkeley: Mizan Press, 1979). See in particular his 'The World-view of Tauhid'.

24. In law and politics, one of those persons who comes closest to this form of thinking is Asaf A.A. Fyzee, *A Modern Approach to Islam* (Lahore: Universal Books, 1978). See especially his 'The Reinterpretation of Islam'.

25. Muhammad Iqbal is one of those who takes this view. See his *The Reconstruction of Religious Thought in Islam* (Dehli: Kitab Publishing House, 1974).

26. This is discussed in C. Muzaffar, 'Al-Quran: Nilai & Peraturan' (the Quran: Values & Rules), *Dewan Budaya*, February and March 1980.

27. This is acknowledged even by a radical feminist like Nawal el-Saadawi. See her *The Hidden Face of Eve*, ed. and tr. Shariff Hetata (London: Zed Press, 1980).

28. See Yusuf Ali, *The Holy Quran*, Sura III: 179.

29. See Kalam Azad, *Tarjumanal-Quran* p. 153.

30. See Hassan Hanafi, *Religious Dialogue and Revolution* (Cairo: Anglo Egyptian Bookshop, 1976), p. 206.

31. This illuminating point has been made by some Sudanese mystics, among them Ustaz Mahmoud Mohamed Taha. See his *The Religion of Man A new Conception of Islam* and *An Introduction to The Second Message of Islam* (pamphlets produced by the Ustaz and his followers, who call themselves the Republican Brothers, in April 1980).

32. This view of rejuvenation in Islam is conveyed in Syed Hussein Alatas, *Kita dengan Islam* (Singapore: Pustaka Nasional, 1978).

Index

(This index is selective, and covers mainly important concepts and topics discussed in the text. The proper names included are those of founders of religions.)